Discover Scotland's History

First published by Oliver & Boyd, 1963
This revised and updated edition published in 1998 by
Scottish Cultural Press
Unit 14, Leith Walk Business Centre,
130 Leith Walk, Edinburgh EH6 5DT
Tel: 0131 555 5950 • Fax: 0131 555 5018
e-mail: scp@sol.co.uk
http://www.taynet.co.uk/users/scp

Publishers' Disclaimer

British Library Cataloguing in Publication Data
A catalogue record for this book is available from the British Library

ISBN: 1 898218 76 5

Printed and bound by Cromwell Press, Trowbridge, Wiltshire

Discover
Scotland's History

A. D. Cameron

Scottish Cultural Press

Preface

This is a book for everyone who wants to learn something about the history of Scotland. It may already be familiar to some of you from your school days as an updated version of *History for Young Scots*, published by Oliver and Boyd in the 1960s. Oliver and Boyd published a second edition in 1980, with a generous collection of illustrations – maps, plans, drawings, paintings and photographs – which, being closely integrated with the text, helped to bring Scotland's past alive and make it easier to understand.

Language teachers from abroad who saw the 1980 edition often told me that its language and style made it exactly the kind of introduction that visitors to Scotland were looking for. No other book of this kind having appeared so far, I have taken the opportunity to update and revise, and bring together the Scottish chapters to form the core of this one extensive book, *Discover Scotland's History*. Many more subjects and events are discussed and new illustrations have been added to make this the most comprehensive, accessible book on Scottish history available. Guidance is given on some of the best places to visit to relive great, or dark, events in Scotland's history or to experience at first hand the ways of life of Scottish people at different times in the past.

With opinion again beginning to call for more Scottish-based studies in schools, a new review has asserted the right of all Scottish pupils to learn about their own history.

Teachers, it is hoped, will find this new, completely updated edition a helpful resource in the classroom. Perhaps the greatest strength of *Discover Scotland's History* is that it offers readers the opportunity of seeing Scotland's history whole, flowing like a river, and changing, all through recorded time. By discovering here what happened in the past, readers will become informed about the background to the present strong feeling of Scottishness and also be more aware of Scotland's place in the modern world.

I am grateful to many people for information and advice and special thanks are due to Robina McGregor for her immaculate word processing; to my son, David, for preparing the text for the publisher; Stephen Gibson for the maps, diagrams and drawings; and Jill Dick and Avril Gray of Scottish Cultural Press for their enthusiasm and professional skill in producing this book.

A.D.C.
Edinburgh, 1997

Contents

Acknowledgements

The author and publishers would like to thank all those who gave of their time in helping trace the numerous copyright holders. We are indebted to the librarians, curators and archivists across the country who have been so accommodating and supportive.

1

Scotland Imagined, Scotland Early

What impressions do people abroad have of Scotland and the Scots? It seems they expect it to be a land of high mountains, perhaps because the northern part of Scotland, and the biggest, is called the Highlands. Indeed, the Highlands are high compared with the landscape of England, for example, but not so very high when they are compared with the Swiss Alps or the Himalayas.

The kilt, and the tartan from which it is made, are recognised abroad as Scotland's national dress. A Scottish tourist overseas, even in a country as far away as China, need not be surprised if he is asked, 'But where is your little skirt?' In the same way, the bagpipe is the musical instrument which is considered to be particularly Scottish. This may be because every Scottish regiment in the British

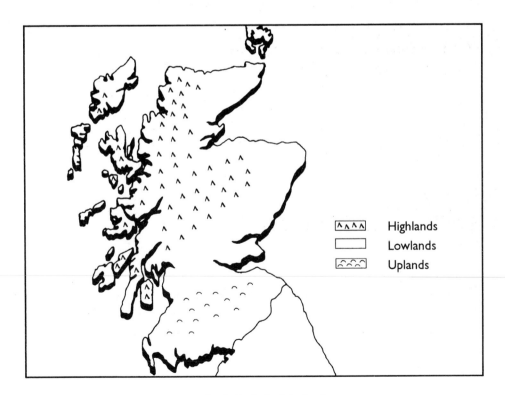

Scotland, the look of the land

army marches to the tunes of its own pipe band or simply because pipe bands have an important role in the life of the nation. They play at Highland Games, for example, at local festivals and at any international event in Scotland in which Scottish teams are taking part.

Scots working abroad and some twenty million people all over the world who have Scottish blood in their veins tend to encourage this image of Scotland. They like to join Caledonian, or Scottish, societies. At Burns Suppers on 25 January each year they meet to pay tribute to the works of Scotland's national poet, Robert Burns, and on St Andrew's Night, 30 November, they remember the patron saint of Scotland. Some people learn to play bagpipes or perform Scottish country dances and may take part in Highland Games. Every year Highland Games are held all over the world, even in Tokyo.

Other nations see the Scots differently. On my only visit to Albania I tried to ask a man the way. Neither of us understood the other's language. 'English?' he asked. 'Yes,' I replied, thinking it was near enough and I was speaking English, 'well, no, Scottish – Ecossais'. 'Ah,' he said and we walked along not saying anything. Then he said something that sounded like 'strawn', then 'stran'. I was puzzled at first and then I guessed. 'Strachan? Gordon Strachan?' I asked and I kicked a stone in the road. His face lit up. 'Gordon Strachan,' he repeated. A few silent paces further on he stopped and said slowly and clearly, 'Kenny Dalglish'.

The Highlands in spring

'Yes, Kenny Dalglish,' I replied and we stuck our thumbs in the air and burst out laughing. He was truly delighted because he had identified the country I came from, a country which is as football-mad as his own. Thanks to television Scotland's international footballers, and rugby players such as Gavin Hastings, are the Scots who are now well known to people abroad.

After spending a few days exploring Scotland, enjoying its scenery and meeting the people, visitors will soon learn what it is really like for themselves.

Scotland Early

Imagine yourself on a deserted island. You are between the sea and the unexplored forest. You begin to feel hungry and think about food. You must look for it. You are in the same position as the earliest visitor to mainland Scotland, who arrived in Fife as early as 5500 BC. He was a food-gatherer. He had most chance of survival on the seashore, where he gathered shellfish. We know this from rubbish heaps (middens) full of shells found on or near the shore. At the right seasons he picked berries, and he collected nuts from the forest.

Hunter with a spear

To get food at other times, he learned to fish and hunt. He caught fish with his hands, or by stunning them with a stone or spearing them with a harpoon made of bone or antler. He would tie a cord to his harpoon to prevent it being carried away downstream. If he ever found a whale washed up on the beach, he and his friends would hack off its flesh with cutting tools made of bone. Except on the windswept north mainland and islands, Scotland was covered by trees. Animals abounded: giant deer, elk, wild oxen, wolves, beavers, lemmings, wildcats, mountain hares, boars, ponies and brown bears. Man learned to make weapons for hunting. Often he was not as strong as the animals he hunted, and he went hunting with other men. Together they made pits to trap animals.

After scraping the inside of animal skins with a sharp stone, folk sewed them into clothes. By rubbing bones down, they made needles for sewing and harpoons for hunting and fishing.

If you strike a piece of flint on a stone you make sparks, and if you use dried moss or fungus or rotten wood or thistle-down as tinder, it will smoulder and burst into flame. You have started a fire with a 'strike-a-light'. Another way of making a fire was by rubbing wood against wood as Boy Scouts have often tried to do. A piece of wood with grooves in it was placed on the ground and a round piece of wood was rubbed vigorously in a groove until the friction made dust and the heat caused the dust to smoulder and catch fire. Making fire in either of these ways was not easy, and when people had a fire going they tried to make sure it never went out.

The discovery of fire completely altered the life of man. People could keep themselves warm, cook their food instead of eating it raw, and ward off wild animals at night. Later they learned to work metals and make weapons by the heat of a fire.

People sheltered in caves, when they could find them. In most places they probably lived in tents of skins, the first man-made homes in Scotland.

No sign of these tent-like dwellings can be seen now, but they are the kind of homes we should expect a hunting people to use (think of the tepees of native Americans). The only traces we have of these people are solid things like stone, bone and pottery made of fired clay, while later people have left their metal tools and weapons. But wood, bark, leather and, later, cloth, must have been just as important in the daily lives of early peoples. From bark alone they could have made baskets and boxes, cradles, shoes, torches, handles for tools and roofs for houses. We cannot find any traces of these now to help us to learn the full story of the people who used them.

Making a fire

2

The First Farmers

In the Near East men made so much progress that they can be considered 'civilised'. Before 3500 BC good crops of grain and flax were being raised on the mud-flats of the Nile delta in Egypt. Further up the river, trenches were dug to carry water to the fields. When the ox-drawn plough was introduced it became possible to grow much more food with far less labour. Egypt became prosperous under the rule of kings called Pharaohs. The royal officials collected taxes and made people obey the laws. They organised a huge force of labourers to control the River Nile and make canals, and to erect public buildings and tombs. The Great Pyramid, for example, which is a royal tomb, is thought to have taken a hundred thousand men about twenty years to build.

At about the same time, settlers were attracted to Mesopotamia, the land between the two great rivers, Tigris and Euphrates, which flow into the Persian Gulf. In addition to growing crops, people kept cows for milk and made cloth from the wool of their sheep. Their rulers had well-equipped and disciplined soldiers, some of whom charged into battle in chariots. Silver money was introduced, and people began to buy and sell goods instead of exchanging one article for another. The value of the money depended on its weight. Skilful smiths made beautiful ornaments from other metals, including gold and copper.

In both Egypt and Mesopotamia people could write. In Egypt they wrote on paper which they made from strips of river reed called papyrus, and in Mesopotamia they cut out the letters on tablets of wet clay. Both civilisations produced a calendar, showing that they could measure time. The Egyptian calendar was the more accurate. It divided the year into twelve months, each with thirty days, and at the end of each year there were five feast days, making a total of 365 days. These are some of the ways in which the peoples of the Near East were more advanced than those in Europe.

New Stone Age People in Scotland

About 3700 BC new people began to settle in Scotland. They came from the shores of south-west Europe in boats hollowed out of tree trunks. They came gradually, hugging the coast, some settling in the south and east of England. Many perished on the way, but the most skilful and the strongest survived. Voyaging through the

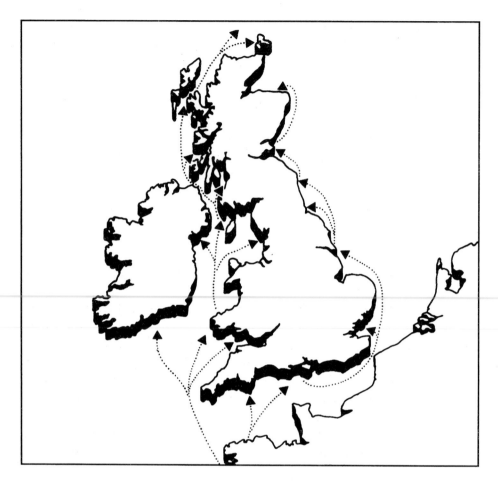

How New Stone Age people came to Scotland

Irish Sea, they reached the western mainland and islands where some remained, while others went farther north to settle in the Shetland Isles. The east coast was settled, too, when the descendants of the people who had made their homes in south-east England came north by sea. We do not know what race they were, because they left no written records. But we know something of their way of life from the materials they used for the best of their weapons, and we call them New Stone Age people.

These people were better equipped to obtain their basic needs than the earlier food-gatherers and primitive hunters had been. They tamed dogs to help them in hunting. They had axes of polished stone, shaped and smoothed. Their cutting and boring tools, however, were not like modern tools, because they did not know how to use metals. Before 3500 BC people elsewhere were already using copper but in Scotland at this time men used lumps of hard stone called 'flint', and split them into flakes.

They made knives, borers, scrapers, daggers and arrowheads out of these flakes, which they sharpened by striking them on the edge with a stone. Among the weapons they used were the bow and arrow. The shaft of the arrow was shaved smooth with a flint knife and scraper, the tail was trimmed with feathers from a bird like the eagle or the goose, and a piece of flint was fixed in the arrow's head. The earliest arrowheads were shaped like a birch or a willow leaf.

If you think that stone tools were not much use, you are wrong. Not long ago a worker in Denmark was given stone tools instead of steel ones. He cut wood, made planks and built a complete house with them by himself in less than twelve weeks.

Living at Skara Brae

Let us take a close-up view of the New Stone Age folk who lived at Skara Brae in Orkney five thousand years ago.

On the sandy shore of the Bay of Skaill on the west coast of Orkney a whale has been cast up by the sea. Men are hacking off chunks of flesh which their womenfolk pile into big whalebone basins. Children chase one another round and over the top of this mountain of flesh. Everyone is chattering, 'Here is food; here is plenty.' The cattle and the sheep are left unguarded on the pastures. No one is hunting for seabirds today and no one is out fishing for cod.

An old man sits on a stone to rest.

'The sea has been good to us,' he murmurs. 'Now no one need starve. There is food here for many moons. Look at these huge bones. Why, we can make new

Skara Brae

supports for our roofs.' He points towards a jumble of connected domes where smoke rises. 'We can make more basins to hold water and milk. Our women will be pleased to have new awls to sew together our clothes of skin. They can boil the blubber and get plenty of oil for cooking. This big skin would make clothes for all of us, but we shall use it to re-roof our houses to keep the rain out. Yes, the sea has been kind.' He picks up his knife of split beach-pebble and returns to help the excited, toiling men.

When they are tired from their labours, they carry the flesh, blubber, bones and skin towards the rising smoke. They seem to be walking into the side of a hill. Perhaps all these people live in the ground. No, they have built their houses at Skara Brae very cunningly. On the ground they have carefully laid flat slabs of stone, and piled more stones on top of them to make square rooms, with the walls sloping slightly inward. As the winds from the sea can blow through walls built without mortar and make the houses cold and draughty, the people pile their rubbish outside the walls until the spaces between the eight huts are almost completely filled in. To go from one house to another they creep along low covered alleys. They may be living in their own midden but they do keep the heat in and the strong winds out.

To enter their huts they have to keep their heads down. Inside, they dump their loads of flesh beside the hearth in the middle of the room, where the peat fire is

What the inside of a hut at Skara Brae might have been like

burning low. The mother sets to work attending to the fire, filling up her cooking pot and setting it on the heat to boil. Soon they are sitting on their beds, happily eating their supper of stew. They have only one room, which is roughly six or seven paces across. (You can compare this with one of your rooms at home or with your whole house.) Whalebones form the rafters for the roof of whaleskin, and there may be a hole in the roof to let smoke out.

All the furniture is made of stone, because few trees grow on the islands. At each side of the fire, at floor level, there is a bed like a box of stone with a canopy of skins over it. The people sleep in these box-beds on top of heather and dried grass, covering themselves with skins. At one end of the room stands a dresser made of stone, holding pots and basins on its shelves. There, and in little cupboards in the walls, the people keep their belongings.

They make beads and dice from bones and from the ivory tusks of the walrus. In one of the houses still remaining at Skara Brae, the smaller bed (almost certainly a woman's) contained beads and also pots with colour in them, which suggests that they decorated themselves – body painting is not a recent custom! Animal bones found in the beds tell us that the family chewed the meat from them in bed.

Theirs were peaceful lives and they had no weapons of war. It was not a human enemy that made the folk of Skara Brae leave, but the sea and sand sweeping in. They left in a hurry, leaving everything as it was, even the beads from a necklace which must have snapped as someone scurried along the passageway to safety.

The settlement of Skara Brae disappeared under a blanket of sand. Now archaeologists, who 'dig for history', have rediscovered it and revealed a clear picture of life in Orkney so many years ago.

Farming

If a hunter is unsuccessful he has nothing to eat. The New Stone Age settlers from Europe, however, had learned to domesticate, or tame, animals, and they brought cattle and sheep with them. The list on page 9 shows that sheep were not native to this country. People now hunted less, because their herds of cattle and sheep made their supply of milk and meat more reliable. It was difficult to keep animals during the cold winter months. Many were killed in autumn. The others were fed on hay, twigs and leaves, seaweed, whalemeat and bark, chopped up and boiled in water. Meat was hung up to dry in the wind to help to cure it.

Stone axes and tools of flint made it easier to cut down trees. Men used to fear the forests, which were dark and full of wild animals, but gradually they conquered them and found that the trees were a useful resource. Wood was valuable for building huts and boats. Often the trees were felled and burned to encourage fresh grass to grow for feeding the herds and to provide new land for growing grain. Men either scattered their seeds and raked them among the wood ash, or they made holes with a stick, put in barley seeds and covered them with soil. They

Grinding corn

made sickles for harvesting by using pitch to fix a row of sharp flints into a wooden handle, and they cut the barley stalks not far below the heads. The best seeds from the year's harvest were kept for sowing the next year.

You may wonder how we know that these people grew barley. Several jars known to have been made in the New Stone Age have marks from barley seeds on them. The seeds must have become embedded in the clay when it was still wet.

People, probably the women, spent about an hour every day grinding the corn into flour by working a rubbing stone backwards and forwards on a big smooth stone called a quern. After mixing the flour with water or milk, they baked bread or cakes on stones warmed by the heat of the fire.

The soil became exhausted after growing crops for three or four years in a row. The people would have to clear new ground and might have to move on, but they were becoming settlers rather than wanderers. Growing crops meant a more certain and better food supply, which in turn meant that fewer people starved and the population increased.

We should not think that the New Stone Age people were very poor and uncivilised. Certainly their needs were simple,

Standing stones at Callanish, Lewis, some looking like a ring of human figures in cloaks facing a great central pillar

Cairnpapple, west of Edinburgh, in winter; a place of burial and ceremony for almost 3,000 years

but they must have produced enough food to allow some men, such as stone masons, to do specialised jobs. The magnificent burial mound of Maeshowe in Orkney, for example, which is even earlier than the Pyramids, must have been built by a large number of skilled craftsmen. They handled stones weighing as much as three tonnes, and built dry-stone walls so carefully that the edges of the stones fitted exactly into one another. Some great chief and his family were buried here.

Proof that New Stone Age people were also great builders in wood came with a surprising discovery in 1976. The burned remains of a huge farmhouse were found at Balbridie on the River Dee. It had been 26 metres long and half as wide, and must have stood 9 metres high. Burned wheat and barley seeds tell us these people were farmers and that these were the crops they were growing in the north-east of Scotland at that time. Tests on the charcoal prove that the fire which destroyed the farmhouse took place about 3700 BC.

Visits

If you are particularly interested in stone buildings erected by early peoples, such as houses, cairns and stone circles, it is worth making the effort to visit Orkney and Shetland in the north. Good examples have survived best on islands, away from industrial and urban development, and have become part of the people's heritage.

3

Makers of Bronze, Weavers of Cloth

Spearhead and arrowheads from the Bronze Age (courtesy of the Trustees of the National Museums of Scotland)

Left on their own, the New Stone Age farmers would have had to wait a long time before one of them discovered metals. While they were working with stone tools, people in lands round the Mediterranean Sea, such as Egypt, had learned to mine copper, smelt it and make tools out of it. Then, about 3000 BC, someone in Europe discovered that when a small quantity of tin was added to copper and heated, bronze, a harder metal, was formed. The Bronze Age had begun. We still use bronze in the present day. Look in your pockets and see if you have any 'coppers'. Pence are made of bronze.

The Bronze Age in Britain from around 2000 BC lasted for a long, long time – about fifteen hundred years. Metal came in gradually but it was not used everywhere, or for everything. Stone axes, for example, were still very useful and men still found that flint made good arrowheads. Later, as the land became more crowded, the weapons men had hunted with began to be used in war.

Ireland had good supplies of gold and copper and some men became skilful metal-workers. They made weapons and tools of bronze which were carried across the sea to be traded with people in Scotland.

Bronze Age Homes

The first settlers to come to Scotland knowing how to work metals were the Beaker people. They came over to the British Isles, including Ireland, from Germany and the Low Countries. Very few signs of their homes have been found here and we do not know very much about their lives. We know them from the way they buried their dead, usually in little coffins with sides of flat stones and a huge stone cover on top. They would put a flint knife or a flint arrowhead and sometimes a decorated clay pot called a beaker, probably filled with drink for the journey to the next world, in with the body.

In the village of Jarlshof, in the south of Shetland, some people lived in four oval houses which they had built solidly with stones. When a stranger entered a house, he found himself in a central room where a peat fire burned. On each side he could see into the little round cubicles (the other rooms) which had walls and roofs of stone. Cattle were kept in the largest room at the far end. Whether or not a hole was left in the roof to let the smoke out, is anyone's guess.

Later on, perhaps about 700 BC, a bronze-smith set up his smithy in a room inside the entrance to one of these houses. Using clay moulds he cast axes and swords. The weapons were exactly like those the smiths in Ireland made. He must have settled down to work at his trade among the people of Jarlshof. Few craftsmen can have worked under greater handicaps, for tin had to be imported from Cornwall and charcoal for the furnace came from the mainland, except when enough driftwood was cast up on the shore.

Bronze Age house at Jarlshof, Shetland, with little rooms and a paved floor

Following well-known sea routes, traders would bring him his raw materials: lumps of copper and tin. They would also bring other things to offer him for the bronze tools and axe heads and spearheads he had made.

Work Women Were Likely To Do

When the women were not cooking or grinding grain, they made their own pottery and cloth. Using clay, they produced many of the things they needed in the home: pots and bowls for cooking and keeping food, ladles and spinning whorls. They shaped the clay with their hands and cooked it in an oven until it was hard.

They made cloth from wool. After plucking the wool from the sheep, they combed it. Then the wool was spun which twisted it to give it strength. To do this the woman held the raw wool wrapped on a stick called a distaff. She pulled out a length of wool and attached it to a stick which had a whorl as a weight on the end. She held this in her other hand and spun the yarn by twisting the stick. Then the yarn was woven into cloth on a simple loom.

In some places blue-petalled flax was grown and harvested to be made into linen. Dyes from plants and berries allowed the cloth to be coloured. For the first time people were wearing clothes which were not made of skin.

Spinning and weaving

4

The Iron Age Celts

When the first Celts arrived about 700 BC, they were armed with swords and axes of bronze. Later Celts had iron weapons. Some travelled north overland while others left the north of England by sea and landed on the banks of the Tweed, Forth and Tay.

They were fierce conquerors, organised in tribes. Their warriors loved fighting and kept a record of the number of men they killed. The ornaments they wore, the decorated trappings on their horses and the quality of their weapons were all signs that these men were proud of their skill in war. Led by their chiefs, they rode in chariots, which were as fearsome in battle then as the tank became in modern wars. Their priests, the Druids, were respected because they were the guardians of the law, poets and advisers to the chiefs. The Celts conquered the local people, whom they forced to work for them.

Many of the farmers had lived in undefended farmsteads, but the unsettled times forced them to build wooden fences to protect themselves. People began to look for safety in high places or behind stone walls. Their settlements became more than simply houses to live in and four different kinds of defended places have been found: hilltop forts, hilltop villages, brochs and crannogs.

Hilltop Forts

A hilltop fort with thick walls of wood and stone

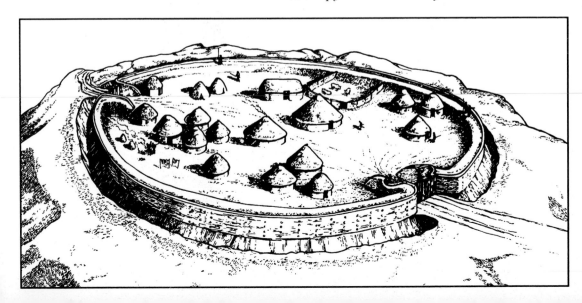

The early forts on hilltops between Inverness and the Tay were defended by walls of stone constructed on a framework of wood. The rampart of the fort at Finavon in Angus (*see* page 27) was over three and a half metres high and nearly twice as wide, stretching for nearly 300 metres round the hilltop. Inside the walls people's houses were round wooden huts on foundations of stone and turf. Later, in Gaul (France), forts like these were named 'Gallic forts' by Julius Caesar.

Hilltop Villages

In the south-east the people also lived in forts on hilltops, or at least above the arable (farming) land. Traprain Law (east of Edinburgh) was a village which was an important tribal capital. It covered an area of thirteen hectares, so it was big enough almost to be called a town. The walls of the round houses were made of wattle and daub; that is, they had a framework of interlaced sticks plastered with clay or mud. The folk there lived by farming and making things. They trained oxen to pull the plough, and prodded them along with sticks with iron tips called goads. The first evidence of a plough has been found at Blackburn Mill in

The Broch of Mousa, Shetland, the most complete in Scotland
(the people on top give the clue to its size)

Berwickshire. The people made and wore woollen clothes. Glass armlets, bronze dress fasteners, pins, brooches and mountings for harness were all made by craftsmen on Traprain Law. These ornaments, and also wool and cloth, were traded with other tribes.

North Eildon, above Newstead (*see* chapter 6), was another tribal capital.

Brochs (first century BC)

The brochs of the north and west were the biggest and most imposing buildings in Scotland before the Middle Ages. They are not found in any other country in Europe. They were great round towers with massive walls of unmortared stones. The entrance was a low tunnel which could be blocked by a stone door. The central courtyard, with a well and an open fireplace, was the scene of day-to-day life and work. It was partly covered over, above head-level, by a lean-to roof, held up by wooden posts. People slept and kept their belongings in little rooms on the ground, feeling secure inside the walls. Inside the broch, they were safe from their enemies. Nobody could climb up the sheer, solid walls and they were too thick to be shattered by a battering-ram.

The brochs were very often built near the sea or a river, and always on good farming land. The people had learned that a field left fallow and used as pasture for animals would soon recover its strength and produce good crops.

Inside a broch

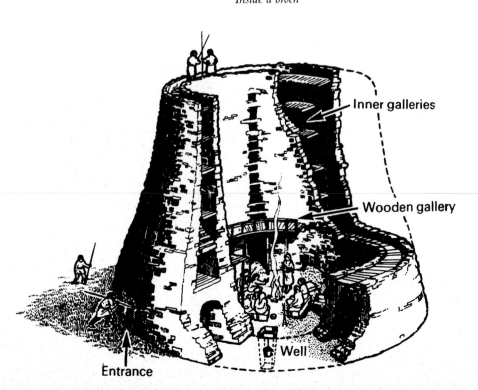

Inner galleries

Wooden gallery

Well

Entrance

Crannogs

Just as some of the Celts looked for safety on hilltops, others in Ayrshire and Galloway, and in big Highland lochs such as Loch Awe and Loch Tay, used surrounding water to protect them. They lived on natural islands in some lochs. More often the islands were man-made, and on each a hut or cluster of huts was erected. These are called crannogs or lake dwellings.

Great wooden uprights were driven into the bed of the loch to give the artificial island its main supports. The uprights were connected by flat beams of oak, through which they fitted like mortised joints. Within this framework layer upon layer of stones, branches of trees, tree trunks and brushwood was placed to raise the island safely above the level of the water. Wooden huts were built on this foundation. At Milton Loch, west of Dumfries, the house was round, walled with logs and thatched with rushes. On the platform round the house the men dried their nets. The fire was inside the house on a hearth of flat stones.

The people had to be able to reach their island homes but try to prevent their enemies from doing so. Usually they made canoes from hollowed-out tree trunks about six metres long and over half a metre deep. Sometimes they made a zig-zagging road under the water, by which a native who knew the way could wade to and from the shore. At Milton Loch, there was a paved causeway.

A crannog

People in the Iron Age

Iron began to replace bronze, not because it made better tools or weapons but because it was easier to produce and much cheaper. With plenty of farm implements like ploughs, hoes and sickles made of iron, land was cultivated more easily and more of the forest was cleared for farming.

Other materials were still used: bone for combs and needles, and for dice for playing a game; stone for pot lids, spinning whorls, querns and lamps; and bronze for jewellery.

Scotland was not united. Many different families and tribes occupied it. Although they built different kinds of homes, they all lived by keeping herds and growing crops. Their chariots (showing their knowledge of the wheel), their pottery and their ornaments, demonstrate that they were not uncivilised, although they were less civilised than the next invaders, the Romans.

A Celtic warrior in his chariot

Visits

The Royal Museum of Scotland, Edinburgh, is a treasure-house of finds from most of the early sites in Scotland, and the capital's exciting new Museum of Scotland opens in Chambers Street in 1998.

To experience a reconstructed crannog in Loch Tay, contact the Scottish Crannog Centre, Croft-na-Caber, Kenmore, Perthshire.

For an opportunity to come close to the lives of people from the earliest times up to the Picts, visit Archaeolink Prehistory Park at Oyne, near Insch, 25 miles north west of Aberdeen.

5

The Romans Come and Conquer

The last great Mediterranean civilisation was that of Rome. Having conquered the Latin farmers of central Italy, the Romans gained control of the whole country. Carthage, a trading city across the sea in North Africa, sent Hannibal and his soldiers to challenge the Romans. They crossed the Alps and advanced almost to the gates of Rome. But the Romans recovered, and wiped out the city of Carthage. During the two centuries before Christ, the Roman legions marched and fought and conquered all the lands round their sea, which they called Mediterranean, 'The Sea in the Middle of the Land'.

Julius Caesar

The great general Julius Caesar conquered Gaul (France) and from there he sighted this land, which he called Britannia, meaning 'The Land of the Britons'. His two invasions, in 55 and 54 BC which first brought Britain into recorded history, were not successful, but they did tell the Britons that Rome existed and was strong.

Not long afterwards, Rome became an Empire under Caesar's nephew, Augustus, who was ruler over Judea when Jesus was born. Nowadays, when we wish to give the date of an event, we say that it took place a certain number of years before or after the birth of Christ. The letters 'BC' beside a date, stand for the words 'Before Christ'. The letters 'AD' mean 'After Christ': they really stand for two Latin words, *anno domini*, which mean 'in the year of our Lord'. So when we say '50 BC', we mean 'fifty years before Christ was born', and when we say 'AD 50', we mean 'fifty years after Christ was born'.

We use the word 'century', meaning a period of one hundred years, when talking about time. All the years from 100 BC to 1 BC, for example, are said to be in the first century BC. All the years between the birth of Christ in AD 1 and the year AD 100 are in the first century AD, and so on.

The Roman Conquest of Britain

The serious conquest of Britain began in AD 43 when the Emperor Claudius sent legions to these shores. The south and east of the country were taken only with difficulty and, while the Romans were trying to conquer the tribes of north Wales, Boadicea, the queen of the tribe of Iceni in the east, led her people in revolt. They recaptured London, burned the town and killed thousands of Romans. However, the Romans did crush the revolt, and then they pushed westwards and northwards.

Agricola

Julius Agricola proved to be a wise ruler and a skilful general when he became governor of Roman Britain.

Once he had conquered the people in the north of Wales, southern Britain became settled. At each of the three big Roman fortresses – York, Chester and Caerleon-on-Usk – a legion of crack troops was stationed, and they built long, straight roads to allow them to move quickly to any trouble-spot. Legionaries from York, for example, could march north along Dere Street to deal with raids by the tribes in the north. South and east of a line between these three fortresses, Britain prospered under Roman rule.

Where there were soldiers, there was money; and where there was money, there was trade. Garrison towns attracted traders, and towns grew up at river crossings, such as London, and at places where roads crossed, such as Lincoln.

The Roman farm was called a villa, and was a large range of buildings, including barracks for the labourers. British landowners built villas like these, and increased their output of food so much that they were able to feed the townsfolk

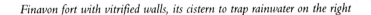

Finavon fort with vitrified walls, its cistern to trap rainwater on the right

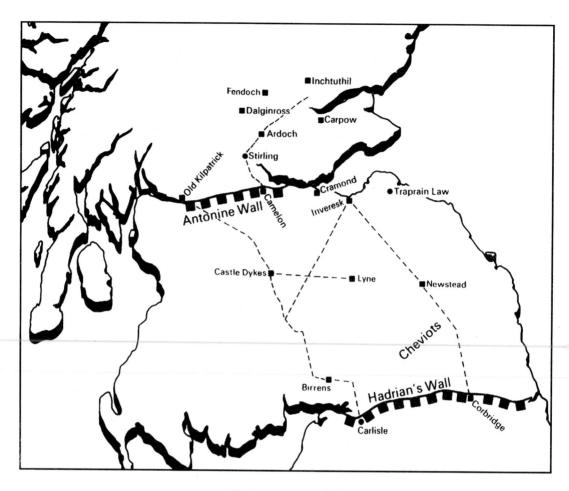

The Romans in Scotland

and the Roman soldiers. New vegetables such as cabbage, beetroot and peas were introduced, and fruit trees like the cherry. British chiefs began to wear the toga, and their sons learned to write Latin. They paid taxes to the Romans, and benefited from *Pax Romana*, or the 'Roman Peace'.

The Romans in Scotland

About AD 80, Roman legions crossed the Cheviots into 'Caledonia', as they called Scotland, and Agricola built a line of temporary forts between the firths of Forth and Clyde. He established more forts north of the Tay, including the great fort at Inchtuthil, which was big enough for an entire legion of 5,000 men. From this base he tried to conquer the North. Some of the hilltop forts, such as Finavon on page 27, are now called 'vitrified forts' because their timber-framed stone walls were burned with such intense heat that the material 'ran together'. The burning used to be blamed on the Romans but excavation has shown that it happened long before the Romans came.

The Celts saw nothing of Roman civilisation, only the damage the Roman soldiers did. 'They make a wilderness and they call it peace,' said Calgacus, a Celtic chief.

In AD 84, Agricola's soldiers fell on the northern tribes at the battle of Mons Graupius. Many of the Celts were killed and the rest driven into the hills. Before Agricola could try to invade the Highlands, however, he was recalled to Rome. But he had made Scotland, south of the Forth and Clyde, part of the Roman Empire.

Later the possibility of raids by the Celts from the north made the Romans decide to withdraw from Scotland altogether. A line between the Solway Firth and the Tyne was chosen by the Emperor Hadrian for building a wall, which was to be the northern limit of the Roman Empire.

Hadrian's Wall

As it stands today, this wall is by far the largest and most spectacular historical ruin in Britain. It stretches more than 112 kilometres from sea to sea. On the north side of it is a deep ditch, and behind it runs a straight road connecting the forts. Built

Hadrian's Wall, with its turrets and milecastles and road behind it (reconstruction by Alan Sorrell, Crown copyright, courtesy of Historic Scotland)

This bit of wall and one turret built up to full height at Vindolanda shows visitors how the wall originally looked

by the Roman soldiers between AD 122 and 128, the wall is two and a half metres wide, faced with dressed stones on either side, and filled in with rubble between the stone blocks. The picture on the left shows it as it used to be with its walls over four metres high.

Along the wall were a series of strong forts, on the same pattern as Newstead (*see* the following chapter) but smaller in size, each being able to house from 500 to 1,000 men. Between them, every 1,000 paces, were 'milecastles', where guards looked out constantly over the bleak moorland for signs of Celts on a raid. The soldiers who manned the wall were not legionaries, but auxiliaries, recruited from tribes all over the Empire: among them were Belgians, Germans and Spaniards.

Hadrian's Wall as it is today

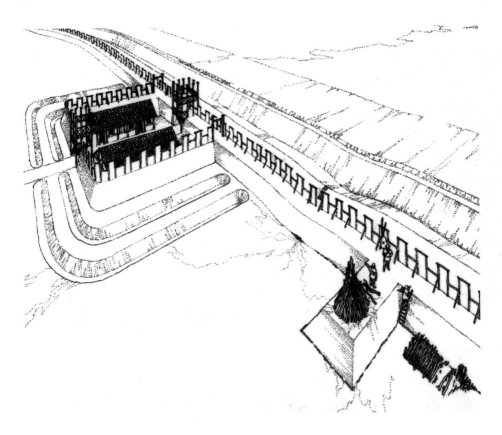

An artist's impression of the Antonine Wall showing the wall and the ditch,
with a small fort on the left and a beacon for sending signals on the right
(by kind permission of David J. Breeze and Michael J. Moore)

The Antonine Wall

In AD 142, the Romans occupied the south of Scotland again, and, as Agricola had
done earlier, they chose the narrowest part between the Clyde and the Forth as the
new frontier. Here they built a new boundary. It was just over half the length of
Hadrian's Wall, running for 60 kilometres from sea to sea. In front was a ditch,
three and a half metres deep and 12 metres wide. Six metres behind it they laid a
foundation of stones, and built square blocks of turf into a huge mound, four and
a half metres at the base, three and a half metres high and nearly two metres wide
at the top. The legionaries did all the work. One of their inscriptions reads: 'In
honour of the Emperor . . . Antoninus Augustus Pius, father of his country, the
Second Legion, Augustus's own, completed [the work of the wall] for 4652 paces'.

At intervals along the wall were 19 forts, roughly one every three kilometres,
and soldiers could move easily from one fort to another along the military road
behind it. Auxiliary soldiers manned these forts.

6

The Roman Soldiers at Newstead

Agricola chose a good position below the three hills which gave the fort its name, Trimontium (now Newstead). It commanded the crossing of the River Tweed to the north of it and stood about halfway between the Tyne and the Forth. The fort, covering an area of six hectares, was the usual shape, square with rounded corners. It had a massive rampart round it, with a stone wall on top, and deep ditches outside it. Outside were other camps and a signal station was built on one of the hills.

Within the defences, the buildings were laid out as shown in this drawing. In the centre were the headquarters of the fort, where the standards and pay-chests

The Roman fort called Trimontium (reconstruction by Alan Sorrell, Crown copyright, courtesy of Historic Scotland)

Brass scales from Roman body armour (courtesy of the Trustees of the National Museums of Scotland)

were kept. On one side was the commandant's house, and on the other the officers' quarters. The commandant's house was centrally heated by a hypocaust, a fire from which hot air passed under the floors and through hollows in the walls. Between them and the headquarters stood the granaries, with their floors raised above ground level to keep the grain dry. To the east were the barracks of the legionaries, the Roman infantry or foot soldiers. The legionaries were Roman citizens. As citizens they could marry or hold property or become officials helping to control the Empire. To the west were the buildings housing the horses and men of the auxiliary cavalry. These auxiliaries, like the men who defended the walls, were not yet Roman citizens.

Work and Weapons

The size and strength of the Roman walls and forts tell us that the Roman soldier spent far more of his time building than he ever did fighting. He had to be prepared to do anything, to build a wall or a barracks, to dig a drain, make roads, store grain or cook the meals. Tools such as hoes, rakes, sickles and scythes, also found at Newstead, are more likely to have been used by native people who cleared the forest, cultivated the soil and grew crops. Some soldiers had special jobs: some worked with leather, making and repairing jerkins, harnesses, boots and shoes; some made armour from fine brass scales, laced together with leather and wire; some made weapons; and some were carpenters. Though all these occupations took up much time, the men were soldiers first and foremost, and would practise fighting for the days when they might march against the Celts or take their turn in guarding the Antonine Wall.

Remains found at Newstead give us a good picture of the Roman soldier. He wore an iron helmet, coming low at the back to protect his neck like a German 'tin hat', and tying under his chin. His jerkin was of leather, and was covered with

*Roman spearhead
(courtesy of the Trustees
of the National
Museums of Scotland)*

iron breastplates curved to the shape of his body, or else with scale armour. The legionary wore breeches which reached halfway down the calf of his leg, and over them he had a skirt which looked like a kilt. His boots were heavy with five or six layers of leather on the soles which had tackets in them.

The legionary carried a short stabbing sword with a blade 50 centimetres long, while the auxiliary had a longer slashing sword. Auxiliaries' shields were normally oval, made of wood-covered leather and bound with bronze. A short bow was used by the auxiliaries to fire arrows, which, for the first time in this country, had iron heads with three barbs. Spears, too, were carried. Often they were quite short ones for throwing, but sometimes they were four metres long.

The bath, on the right of the drawing on page 32, was for the legionaries only. After taking a warm bath, they went into a sweating-room which was filled with hot air, and then into a hot bath. Finally, they had a cold plunge to cool off. They did exercises afterwards, and were massaged by attendants who rubbed ointments into their skin. They played games here too. Gaming pieces, like draughts and dice, have been found, and one soldier left a brooch behind.

Romans and Natives

The Romans held Newstead for two periods, the first lasting until about AD 100. It used to be thought that the Romans were driven out from the fort by a great attack by the Celts, but in the last ten years excavators at Newstead have found few signs of damage. The Roman withdrawal to the line between the Solway and the Tyne seems to have been orderly, with surplus equipment, some of it heavy, like stone querns, helmets and blacksmith's tools, first being hidden from view in wells and pits.

When the Romans returned, about AD 140, they rebuilt the fort, but did not find the treasures their old comrades had hidden. Roman troops were stationed there for over 20 years. The fort became a supply centre for other forts along the Antonine Wall, with fewer soldiers but native craftsmen working inside the fort in workshops, forges and kilns, making weapons and pottery. In the enclosures outside the walls, which can be seen on the plan on page 32, more native people made a living as craftsmen or traders or by growing food for the soldiers. Early this century, archaeologists dug up Newstead fort and found an altar, jugs, beads and coins among the skeletons of unburied animals and men. The Romans had again decided to seek shelter on the south side of Hadrian's Wall.

Their stay in the south of Scotland did not, as it did in southern Britain, result in the wide spread of Roman civilisation. It was a military conquest, achieved by force and maintained by force. Their last attempt to conquer Scotland had not lasted long, and the land fell back into the hands of the Celts, although the Romans controlled the south of Britain for two more centuries. Only their roads lasted and were used by traders for hundreds of years afterwards. Even today, the roads from Carlisle to Glasgow, and from Jedburgh to Dalkeith, follow the routes chosen by the Romans for many kilometres.

Sign on part of the Roman road close to the A68, the road from Jedburgh to Dalkeith

Visits

Most of the material which was found on the Antonine Wall is in the Hunterian Museum at Gilmorehill, University of Glasgow. The collection from the Roman fort at Newstead is in the Royal Museum of Scotland, Edinburgh, and the Trimontium Exhibition on the lives of Romans and natives at Newstead, in the Square, Melrose, is highly recommended.

The Eildons, the same three hills, Sir Walter Scott's favourite view

7

The Making of Scotland

A period of four hundred years, almost as long as the time since John Knox and Mary Queen of Scots, is a remarkable time for any empire to last, especially when it is ruled from a single city. Neither Rome, nor even the whole of Italy, could find enough young men to defend it. More and more of the conquered peoples were joining the Roman armies, until not even the generals were of Roman birth. The Roman Empire had become too big, its thousands of civil servants too great a burden. Great men struggled for power and the poor strove to keep their families and pay their taxes. The Empire did not collapse because of a revolution inside its borders, but because it could not fight off a new threat from outside.

The Barbarians

It is difficult at first glance to see how Britain could be affected by things happening in eastern Asia. At that time, however, the grasslands there began to dry up, and this set the people, the Huns, on the move. Prevented from going east by the Great Wall of China which had been built to keep them out, these fierce, yellow-skinned, black-haired men turned their shaggy ponies towards the setting sun and swept all before them. The movement of the peoples was on! Fearless horsemen, firing bone-tipped arrows as they rode, crossed the Urals and the Steppes of Russia. Unable to stand against these cruel conquerors, some of the Germanic tribes, called Goths, asked to be allowed to settle inside the Roman Empire. Later waves of Goths were to form the new kingdoms in the west: the West Goths in Spain, the East Goths in Italy, the Franks in France.

The Romans tried to face the new danger by giving up their more distant lands like Britain and bringing their forces nearer home. But the capital was captured by Alaric the Goth in AD 410, and the greatness of Rome was at an end.

The Making of England

Britain was now open to attack. The peoples of the lower Rhine valley (the Angles, Saxons and Jutes) were caught up in this movement westwards.

Leaving their villages, the separate tribes of Angles, Saxons and Jutes gathered

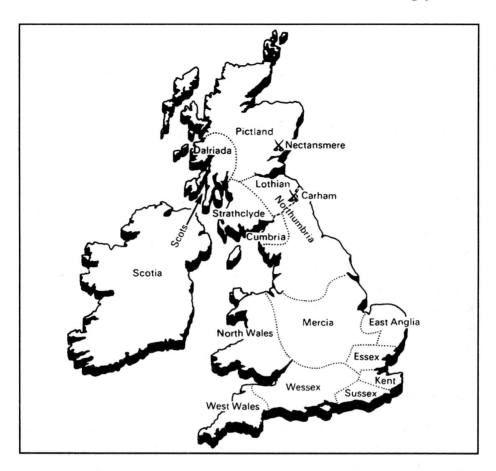

Early kingdoms in England and Scotland

their weapons and rowed across the North Sea in open boats. They were keen seamen who looked on a shipwreck as a good way of gaining experience.

They swarmed round the river mouths, going as far inland as possible before landing. If you look at an atlas, you will notice that most rivers in Britain flow towards the east, making invasion from Europe easier. The invaders fought the Britons on landing, driving them slowly westwards into the highlands of Cornwall, Devon, Wales and the Lake District. They looted and destroyed the Roman forts and towns. Not used to town life, the Anglo-Saxons settled on the banks of rivers or cleared the forests and built villages and cultivated fields as they had done in Germany. They were ruled by small kings but gradually the number of their kingdoms was reduced to three: Northumbria (north of the Humber), Mercia (in the Midlands) and Wessex (occupied by the West Saxons). By the tenth century these were united into Angle-land or 'England'. The newcomers brought their own language: English.

In Wales today many people still speak their own language, Welsh, which is

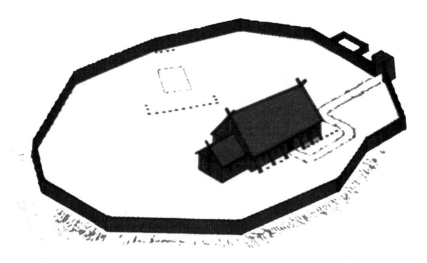

*Seventh-century timber hall on Doon Hill in East Lothian, home of a chief among the Angles
(drawing on the Historic Scotland information board)*

derived from the common speech of the ancient Britons. It may surprise you to learn that the same language also used to be spoken in Scotland by the Britons of Strathclyde.

Four Peoples in Scotland

The movement of the peoples affected Scotland too. North of the Forth the people were called the Picts or 'painted men' by the Romans, from their habit of painting their bodies. We do not understand their language, but we do know that they were fierce warriors, who attacked the Romans in the south. They have left ample proof that they had artists among them because they carved figures of animals, horsemen and foot soldiers on flat slabs. The Picts covered by far the largest area of the country, but much of it was mountainous and the people were widely scattered. In the south-west were the Britons of Strathclyde whose capital was on Dumbarton Rock.

So far, we have used the word 'Scotland' to describe the country, but we have said nothing about Scots. We have, in fact, been describing Scotland before the Scots. Two new peoples now arrived: the Angles from the east, sailing up the Forth and Tweed, and the Scots from the west. The Angles drove the native Britons westwards into Galloway and the Clyde valley. The Scots came over in skin-covered boats from Ireland to settle in Dalriada in Argyll. They spoke Gaelic and they introduced the Gaelic language to Scotland. In time, their small kingdom, though cut off from the rest of the country by mountains, was to give its name to the whole people.

Let us consider how these four peoples were united. There can be no doubt that the spread of the Gospel by the followers of Ninian and Columba gave them all something they shared which was stronger than the mountains or the different languages which divided them. But it was not certain then that Scotland as we know it would ever become an independent kingdom. The Angles of Northumbria controlled most of the land from the Humber to the Forth, and swept northwards into Pictland. In AD 685, however, 'God favoured Brude mac Bile'. This Pictish king and his warriors overwhelmed the Angles at Nectansmere near Forfar. His great victory made sure that the land, north of the Tay at least, would remain independent.

In AD 843, Kenneth MacAlpin, King of Scots, became king of the Picts as well. He seems to have had a claim to the Pictish throne through his mother. This was at a time when more Scots were coming over from Ireland while the Picts were suffering from Viking raids. This explains why the Scots triumphed and the country became 'Scotland' and not 'Pictland'.

The lands between the Forth and the Cheviots became part of the northern kingdom by the middle of the eleventh century. The Angles of Lothian in the east were certainly under the rule of King Malcolm II of Scotland by 1018, after his

Close to Nectansmere, the Aberlemno Stone's scenes from the battle with the Picts on the left, chasing a fleeing horseman (top), on foot against an armed horseman (middle), and on horseback (bottom) with a raven, the symbol of death

victory over the English at Carham-on-Tweed. Sixteen years later, Malcolm was succeeded as king by his grandson, Duncan, king of the Britons of Strathclyde. Duncan I was the first king to rule over the whole of Scotland, as we know it, except for the north and west which were in the grip of the Vikings (*see* chapter 9).

Early Peoples and the Names of Places

NAME	LANGUAGE	MEANING	PLACE
Pit	Pictish	bit of farmland or farm steading	*Pittodrie* (croft by the wood, or, on the slope) *Pitlochry* (stony piece of land)
Bal	Gaelic	village	*Ballindalloch* (village in the field) *Ballachulish* (village on the straits)
Kil	Gaelic	church	*Kilbride* (church of St Brigid)
Caer	British	fort	*Caerlaverock* (fort of the lark)
Pen	British	hill	*Penpont* (hill by the bridge)
Ton	English	village	*Swinton* (Swein's toun)
Ham	English	home or village	*Tyninghame* (village of the people by the River Tyne)

Curraghs: lightweight boats which probably carried the Scots to Argyll, photographed in Ireland

8

The Coming of Christianity

He died that we might be forgiven,
He died to make us good.

In the nineteenth century many people went
out to Africa or India to be missionaries. They
lived among the people there, teaching the
children, healing the sick and telling them about
the life and the example of Jesus Christ and his
death on the cross. In the early centuries after
the birth of Christ, people here had not heard
the Gospel, the 'good news'. *They* were the
heathen peoples, and the missionaries came to
them.

We know little about the religion people
followed in early times. The people were
mystified by the world around them, and
worshipped what they welcomed but did not
understand. Led by the Druids, they
worshipped the rising sun, the giver of light and
warmth. Some of the things people do today at
Beltane feasts and Hallowe'en have survived
from early religions.

St Ninian

Ninian grew up among the Britons and went to
France to be educated. He was eventually made
a bishop in Rome. Inspired by the great St
Martin of Tours in France, he learned to go
away on his own at times to think and pray, and
then to return to the world to spread the word
of God. When he returned to live among the
Britons in the fifth century, some of them were

*St Martin's Cross, Iona
(courtesy of Norman Glen)*

probably already Christian. He became the first religious leader whose name is known in Scotland. He and his helpers worshipped in St Martin's Church at Whithorn in Galloway. With its walls covered in white plaster, it was known as the 'white house'. In these headquarters they prayed and worked together. Local chiefs sent their sons to school there and young missionaries came to be trained. Dressed in cloaks of undyed wool and carrying a book and a staff, the missionaries set out to preach to the people in the hilltop forts, working their way north. An early church at Eccles (the word means 'church') is dedicated to St Ninian, and there is another in Glasgow. Later on, churches built in his name appear at Dunottar and Methlick in Aberdeenshire, and Navidale in Sutherland.

Many places have a connection with a local saint. Glasgow, the 'green hollow', claims St Kentigern (Mungo); Culross in Fife has St Serf, whose retreat (or 'desert') was at Dysart which sounds much the same. Edinburgh and some Border towns claim St Cuthbert. Often the oldest church, the parish church, is dedicated to St Mary, but the names of other churches sometimes provide clues to local saints.

The decorated capital 'S' and letters of the Latin for 'But neither' from The Book of Kells

St Columba

The Scots, you will remember, came from Ireland. It was also from Christian Ireland that Columba came, not as a young man dedicated to the Church, but as a monk of royal birth disgraced in his own country. A quarrel over who owned a copy of the Psalms which he was making led to a battle which drove him to exile himself. In AD 563, he set out to find a place far from the shores of Ireland.

He and his twelve companions pushed off in their boats in the same direction as their fellow Scots had gone, towards Dalriada. Tossed like corks on the Atlantic waves, they came at last to the windswept island of Iona, off the west coast of Mull. Here was a place of loneliness and silence, yet near enough to the Scots of

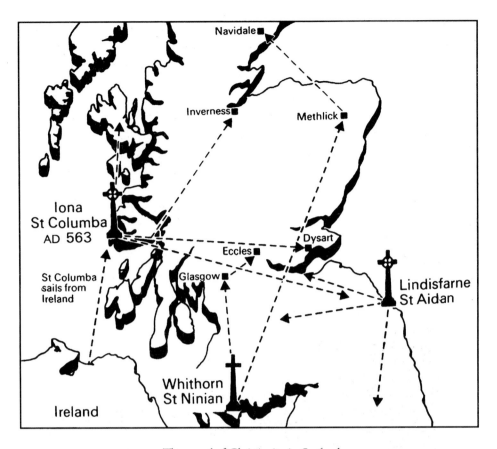

The spread of Christianity in Scotland

Dalriada, and here they built their church. They were a simple, self-supporting community, living in separate huts round the church, with only such other buildings as were necessary. There was the kitchen, the guest-house (for they made a 'fuss' of strangers), the stable, the workshop and the granary. They kept flocks of sheep, ploughed the land and fished. Like the followers of St Ninian they lived humbly, having nothing to call their own. Columba himself, we are told, had only a stone for a pillow.

They loved learning. After all, Columba had left Ireland because of the secret copy he had made of the Psalms. Lovingly they copied the sacred words of the Gospels. An example of their work, which was begun on Iona, is the beautiful *Book of Kells*, now in Trinity College, Dublin. The standard of decoration was very high, as you can see from the illustration opposite, and writing was tiring and difficult, as the monk who wrote these words tells us:

My hand is weary with writing
My sharp quill is not steady

My slender-beaked pen pours forth
A black draught of shining dark-blue ink.

They paddled their little boats to northern islands like Skye. They went up the long sea lochs, and travelled across Perthshire and Fife, bringing to the Picts the story of Christ. Columba himself, fearless of robber and wolf, reached Inverness, where he may have converted King Brude as well as some of the Picts.

For years Columba and his disciples made Iona the religious centre of the north. He was a strong, rugged commanding figure, but at the same time a kind, friendly man, who loved children and animals. When he was very old, and knew that he was going to die, he climbed the slope above the church and blessed the island with these words:

Unto this place, small and mean though it be, great homage shall yet be paid, not only by the kings and peoples of the Scots, but by the rulers of barbarous and distant nations with their people. Thy saints also, of other churches, shall regard it with no common reverence.

Statue of St Cuthbert at Lindisfarne, Holy Island, Northumberland

So indeed they have, and with reason. Christianity, being shared by the Picts and the Scots, helped them to join together as one nation. St Aidan left Iona and made Lindisfarne (Holy Island) his home for his work in converting Northumbria (which included what is now south-east Scotland). To carry on Aidan's work, St Cuthbert left his sheep on the Lammermuir hills to tend a human flock.

Most of England, however, received the Gospel later from St Augustine and his followers, who had come from Rome. Roman Christianity in southern England and eventually (by the decision taken at the Synod of Whitby in AD 664) in Northumbria as well, helped to unify the English, and to separate them from the northern peoples, the children of Whithorn and Iona.

St Andrew with his cross, as depicted on a window in the parish church, Douglas, Lanarkshire

St Andrew

'Why,' you may ask, 'is St Andrew the patron saint of Scotland?' This is the reason. Andrew, the first of Jesus's disciples, was crucified on a saltire, or X-shaped cross, in Greece. Some of his bones were carried to a church in what is now the town of St Andrews in Fife, and this church became the most important in Scotland. St Andrew's Day, 30 November, is remembered as Scotland's special day, particularly by Scots abroad, and his cross has become the national flag.

Visits

Visitors may want to explore Iona, the island of St Columba; or visit Whithorn for St Ninian, whose cave, his place for quietness and prayer on the edge of the sea, marks the end of the modern Pilgrims' Way; or you can follow St Cuthbert's Way from Melrose Abbey to Holy Island, off the Northumberland coast.

9

The Vikings

It is high tide on Iona, on a summer morning in the year 806.

A shepherd looks out to sea, attracted by the screeching of sea birds. There's a boat with a sail, another and another – eight in all – riding proudly on the waves. He peers into the distance in fear. Can it be . . . ? He sees the raven on the sail of the foremost ship. The Vikings are coming, the demons, the plunderers, the killers. He runs through the heather, down the slope to the church.

'They're coming, they're coming!' he screams. The brothers understand at once. There have been raids before.

The bell tolls. The abbot tries to comfort the monks and leads them in prayer. He orders the ornaments and precious writings to be hidden, and walks out to meet the invaders. They are landing now from their long, narrow boats, which they have drawn up high on the sand. Look at them – tall men, fierce men, all with round shields, terrifying battle-axes and swords. The abbot stands before them, pleading with them to leave his church in peace. They brush him aside, and rush to the

Vikings landing

Viking weapons (photograph by Ernst Schwitters; by kind permission of the Department of Archaeology, Numismatics and History of Art, Oslo)

settlement. Some make for the byre, drive the cows down to the shore and kill them there for food. Most of them hurry into the church. They catch the monks storing their treasures under stone slabs. Axes swing, swords flash and monks fall dead. With straw and a light the church is set on fire. The brethren outside kneel and pray, but they are put to the sword. Sixty-eight people on the island become martyrs, and the Vikings go back to their ships, laden with treasures and supplies.

The Vikings as Sailors

Who were these invaders whom we have called Vikings and how and why had they come?

They were great sea warriors, who came from Scandinavia. If you look at a map of Scandinavia, made up of Norway, Sweden and Denmark, you will see that much of it is mountainous, and that the west coast is cut into by a great many fiords. In the time of the Vikings the hill-land was poor, so that the men looked to

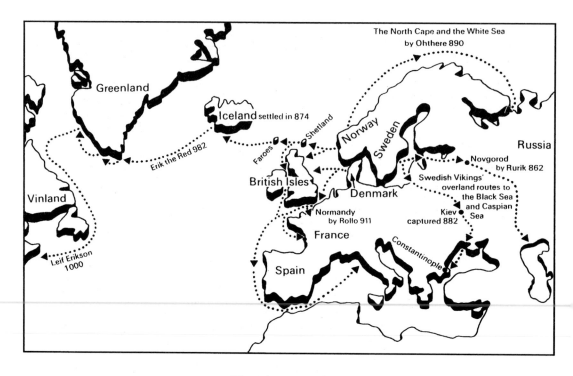

The North Cape and the White Sea
by Ohthere 890

Greenland

Iceland settled in 874

Shetland

Norway

Sweden

Russia

Erik the Red 982

Faroes

Novgorod
by Rurik 862

British Isles

Swedish Vikings'
overland routes to
the Black Sea
and Caspian
Sea

Vinland

Denmark

Normandy
by Rollo 911

Kiev
captured 882

Leif Erikson
1000

France

Constantinople

Spain

The Vikings as explorers

the sea for a living. Having discovered how to make iron, they made tools to cut down trees and used the wood to make boats. They fished, but soon the sea beckoned them further and they became explorers and raiders.

Their boats were long and wide but could be sailed in shallow water and could be hauled up on a beach on a summer raid. Often decorated with the head and tail of a dragon, they were driven by oars and one large sail. Their side rudder made them easy to steer on long sea voyages.

On their early expeditions, the Vikings sailed to plunder other lands. Naturally, the best places to raid, in their eyes, contained not only food, drink and clothing, but also gold and silver ornaments to take back to their womenfolk.

The St Ninian's Isle treasure – 28 silver bowls and brooches – was discovered under the floor of a little church in Shetland by a boy in 1958. It probably belonged to a chief who had it stored there for safety. This may be another reason why holy places suffered so many attacks, and why the monks feared the Vikings and welcomed the bad weather, as an Irish monk tells us in the margin of his manuscript:

> The bitter wind is high tonight;
> It lifts the white locks of the sea.
> In such wild winter storm no fright
> Of savage Viking troubles me.

The Vikings returned home to spend the winter building boats, making weapons, eating, drinking and telling stories in their halls high above the fiords. Their love of adventure and their feeling for the sea made them great sailors and explorers. They knew nothing of the compass, although they sailed in their great ships to new lands – Shetland, Orkney, the Faroes, Iceland and Greenland. Usually they sailed westwards, reaching out towards the setting sun. They found their way by using rough-and-ready rules. Sailing to Greenland, for example, they passed the Faroes at a distance from which the sea appeared halfway up the mountains. They sailed south of Iceland at a distance from which wildfowl and whales could be seen, and westwards to a point in Greenland just north of Cape Farewell. It is interesting to follow this voyage of the Vikings on a map.

The Vikings as Settlers

Erik the Red discovered Greenland and settled there. His son, Leif Erikson, was the first man to sail direct from Greenland to Norway and back. Later, about AD 1000, Leif sailed along the coast of North America, which he called Vinland. This was nearly 500 years before Columbus 'discovered' America.

Viking village at Jarlshof, Shetland (reconstruction by Alan Sorrell, Crown copyright, courtesy of Historic Scotland)

For centuries the Vikings searched for lands which were like their own but better, where they could live in the same way but make a living with less effort. They became land-winners or settlers. Under the leadership of Rurik, they entered and gave a name to Russia; under Rollo they occupied Normandy, the land of the Northmen in France; under Guthrum and later kings Sweyn and Canute, they settled in England. Shetland, Orkney, Caithness and Sutherland, the Hebrides, Ireland, the Faroes, Iceland and Greenland all became Viking lands, and the North Atlantic almost a Viking lake.

The Viking *Sagas* tell of the hardships they faced and the heroic deeds they performed while conquering these new lands. They tell us who the foremost Vikings were. Some warriors were given surnames which described their looks: Harold Fairhair, Erik the Red, Helgi the Lean and Onund Woodenleg; some their dress: Ragnar Hairy-breeks and Magnus Bareleg; and some because of their reputation in battle: Erik Bloodaxe and Thorfinn Skullsplitter.

They were not merely destroyers. They kept their links with the sea by pirate

*A reconstruction of a Viking longship alongside a restored fishing boat
in Lerwick Harbour, Shetland*

raids and slave-trading, but they fished as well, and even used boats for moving crops of hay. They settled in lonely parts of Scotland like Jarlshof in Shetland.

Jarlshof was as attractive to the Vikings as it had been to Stone Age and Bronze Age peoples up to 3,000 years earlier. The land was fertile, and there were cod to catch and grey seals to hunt. Besides, Viking ships often called there from Orkney on the way to Norway, only 48 sailing hours away.

Their homes were longhouses, each one longer than a cricket pitch. The walls were thick, each like two 'dry-stane dykes' side by side, with earth packed in between them. Driftwood was cut up to form low-ridged roofs which were covered with heather, straw or sometimes peat. Stones tied to straw ropes over the thatch kept it secure in the high winds.

The oldest house at Jarlshof, probably the headman's, contained a large living-room, with a fire in the middle, and a smaller room (the kitchen) where food was cooked in an oven by the heat of stones taken out of the fire. The house was smoky, and peat soot covered the rafters. The other houses had people and animals living under the same roof. They were 'clarty but cosy'. The outbuildings included a byre, a barn and a smithy, where a hole worn five centimetres deep in a stone anvil is proof that the smith was always hammering on it, making everything from sickles to fishing-hooks. People walked along paths of stone slabs, and in the yard there were stone platforms on which hayricks stood.

Their work changed with the seasons. There was sowing in the spring, followed by lambing, sheep-shearing, hay-making, harvesting barley and slaughtering some of the animals before winter set in. They cut peats and dried them in the sun on the hill across the bay. They enjoyed fishing in summer. The sheep-shearing saw the start of another year's cloth-making. Washing, combing and spinning followed one after another until, during the winter evenings, they were ready to weave the wool on an upright loom by the light of little oil lamps. All the year round there were the cattle, sheep and pigs to herd, and in the winter the cows were kept indoors in byre-stalls. The men killed many calves, lambs and young pigs for food. They caught fish and killed seabirds to get something different to eat. Usually they ate flesh and fish only, bread being kept for feasts.

These crofter-fishermen at Jarlshof were typical of thousands of Vikings who settled on the mainland and islands of Scotland, bringing with them their knowledge of sea-faring and boat-building. The dialects and names of places in the northern islands show how far they spread. For centuries they were a threat to Scottish kings, but they did bring courage, strength and a spirit of adventure to Scotland.

Visit

For the saga of the Vikings in Scotland, visit Vikingar! in Largs on the coast of Ayrshire (*see* chapter 16 for the Battle of Largs).

10

Malcolm Canmore and St Margaret

By the time of the reign of Malcolm III (1057–93), Scotland was a united country, covering roughly the same area as today. True, the islands and north mainland were subject to the Vikings, but elsewhere the king's word was law. Though the people recognised Malcolm Canmore[1] as king, it is doubtful if they thought of themselves yet as one nation. Local chiefs still had great power. Not all the people spoke the same language. Pictish was dying out, and Gaelic was becoming the language of the Highlanders. In the south of Scotland, English was spoken in the east and was coming to be used in the west. There were also differences in religion, because not all Scotland had been converted by St Columba.

Malcolm Canmore

With so many races in Scotland, it is not surprising that Malcolm's own background was mixed. Half Celtic, half English, he 'had the Gaelic' and spoke

Scene from the Bayeux Tapestry (eleventh century) showing Harold under his name,
wounded by an arrow in his eye, and to the right cut down by a horseman's sword
(by special permission of the City of Bayeux)

English as well. His father, Duncan, had been killed by Macbeth, but not murdered by him, as Shakespeare's play would have us believe. When Macbeth seized the throne, Malcolm had to flee to England for safety. In the south he learned how England and the other countries in Europe were ruled. There, too, although Malcolm was never able to read or write, he had met and admired men of learning. Finally he returned to Scotland and defeated Macbeth at the battle of Lumphanan in Aberdeenshire. He became king of Scotland, and set up his capital at Dunfermline.

The Norman Conquest of England

While Malcolm was king in Scotland, England was successfully invaded from Europe. The Normans, who were descendants of the Vikings, had settled in Normandy in France, where they became Christian and learned to speak French. Training and practice made them skilled fighters on horseback. Led by their duke, William, they came across and defeated the English at the Battle of Hastings in 1066, and William became king of England. The story of the invasion is shown in pictures in a magnificent piece of needlework made in England soon afterwards. Called the Bayeux Tapestry, it is now in Bayeux in Normandy, France.

Harold, the king of the English, had been killed at Hastings. Edgar, the English heir to the throne, had to flee from the Normans with his family including his sister, Margaret. They came north by sea, and landed on the south coast of Fife, in a bay between Rosyth and North Queensferry, which is now known as St Margaret's Hope. Malcolm made the refugees welcome at Dunfermline, and Margaret became his second wife and queen.

St Margaret

Margaret must have seemed to the Scots a strong-willed woman who had very expensive tastes. She delighted in the 'show' of royalty. When the king travelled she saw that he was always escorted by a strong bodyguard on horseback. She made the royal palace a blaze of coloured fabrics and decked the royal table with gold and silver dishes and goblets. Her demands encouraged trade, especially in luxuries.

It should not be thought that Malcolm had married a queen who dominated him and imposed her own foreign will on Scotland. He was a rough, tough warrior whose army invaded the north of England time and again, often with great cruelty. They wanted to make Scotland more modern and more religious, and tried to govern it better. Together they took the best of what they knew of Europe as their model. Certainly, she helped him to rule the country, the first woman to take part in governing Scotland.

---

[1] *Canmore* was Malcolm's Gaelic nickname. It meant 'Great Head' or 'Chief'.

Had she not married, Margaret would have entered a convent and become a nun. A sincere and very religious woman, she did all she could to help the poor. Her ladies learned that she disapproved of riotous laughter. They copied her gracious manners and followed her example in doing good. Margaret did all she could to help the church in Scotland. She invited the first monks to come to Dunfermline, and they began to build the great abbey there. She also provided houses for pilgrims to stay in on either side of the Forth, and they could cross the river on the Queen's Ferry free of charge on their way to St Andrews.

On hearing the news of Malcolm's death during another attack on the north of England, Margaret died in Edinburgh Castle, where her small chapel still stands. Her tomb lies beside that of her husband in Dunfermline Abbey which has been a place of pilgrimage since 1250 when Margaret became Scotland's first, and only, royal saint.

Visits

St Margaret's Chapel in Edinburgh Castle and Dunfermline Abbey are worth visiting.

St Margaret's Chapel, built on a rock, in Edinburgh Castle

11

David I and Norman Ways

Although William had been crowned king of England, he still needed men to fight against the English until he controlled the whole country. Then he had to reward them. He did this not with money, but with land. Norman lords were given areas of land if they swore to obey the king and bring a fixed number of knights to fight for him when he needed them. In this way, a lord became the king's tenant (from the French word *tenir*, to hold), holding land in return for military service. Lords who held land directly from the king were called tenants-in-chief. They did not normally wish to keep a great number of knights in their own houses. So they kept a large piece of land for themselves, and gave the rest to their tenants. These men swore an oath of homage, to become 'the lord's man' and promised to bring a smaller number of knights for the king. They might divide up their lands, too, keeping part for themselves and splitting the rest between their knights. Holding land like this is called 'feudalism'.

There were a number of ways in which the Normans differed from the English. They were foreigners who spoke French. They had gained land and become a new landed aristocracy. They ruled over the English. Roughly speaking, they were the lords and knights, and the English became serfs and had to work for them. They were knights, trained to fight on horseback. For protection they wore a hauberk, a long leather coat covered by metal rings, with slits at the back and front to allow them to sit comfortably on their horses. Their helmets were cone-shaped, with a strip of metal coming down in front to protect the nose. The lance was their chief weapon but they carried swords as well. They occupied castles at important places, to keep the English down. They even looked different, with their shaved chins and their hair cut short at the back and sides.

David, Earl of Huntingdon

To avoid the trouble in Scotland after the deaths of Malcolm and Margaret, their younger children were sent to England to be brought up. David went to the court of William Rufus, where he became a scholar and a knight. This is important in Scottish history because David brought back many of the latest European ideas from England.

David was Earl of Huntingdon in England, and had other lands as well. He was

*Arms of Robert the Bruce's family as earls
of Carrick in Ayrshire*

one of the chief nobles at the court and a trusted adviser of the next English king, Henry I. David saw from the inside how a good king ruled. He learned a lot.

David and the Normans

The Normans had come to England as invaders and stayed on because they had conquered it. Scotland suffered no Norman conquest. The Normans came north because David invited them. When he became King of Scots, he brought some of his Norman friends with him. Many of their names are common names in Scotland today: names like Bruce, Lindsay, Montgomery, Graham and Somerville. Normans who followed them included Melvilles, Fairbairns, Archibalds and Ramsays. Walter Fitz Allan, who gained lands in Renfrewshire, became the royal Steward, and from this came the surname Stewart and ultimately a royal line.

Feudalism in Scotland

In parts of Scotland, as in England, feudalism was introduced. The newcomers were given land, on condition that they brought knights to fight for David. For example, an early Robert de Brus (Bruce) was given Annandale in return for the service of ten knights. He swore an oath of homage to the king, promising 'to be his man' and another of fealty, like this:

> I, Robert, swear on these holy Gospels of God that henceforth I shall be faithful to you, as a vassal ought to be to his lord. You will never lose life or limb, nor the honour you have, by my will, advice, or encouragement, but in all those things I shall be your helper according to my power.

This suited the king. In return for the land they held, the lords all promised to obey him. Notice that they did not own the land, for it was all the king's: they 'held' it. Even today, by the law of 'treasure trove' in Scotland, anything found on or in the ground belongs to the Crown. 'What belongs to no one belongs to the king.' Each lord kept his own men in order. From the king's point of view, it helped him to rule the country, and it gave him horsemen for his army without having to pay them.

The king would go to the lands he granted and pace out or ride the limits, pointing out boundary marks like 'the old oak tree', or 'the big round stone', since there were no maps. Details of the land he was giving and the services the tenant was to give were written down on a charter, which was signed and sealed before witnesses. This was the lord's legal title to his land. It was also the first sign that the king was having letters written by his civil service. These men were all churchmen, because they were the only people who could write.

Churches and Castles

The land of a lord or tenant became known as his domain. Near its centre was his tower or fortified house. A church was built close by and it served the parish, which was usually the same size as the lord's domain. With the lord to protect him, the priest collected the tithes, the tenth of every man's produce from the land which was due to the Church to keep the priest and the poor. The finest existing Norman parish church in Scotland, at Dalmeny, near Edinburgh, has typical Norman rounded arches over its door and windows.

The king built castles in many places. Wherever there was a royal castle David would place a Norman baron to be his sheriff, to maintain law and order in the surrounding countryside. This area became a shire, with the castle, and later the

Dalmeny Church with round arches over its doorway and windows, probably the finest Norman church in Scotland

town which grew up beside it, as its centre or capital. The sheriff was also in charge of defending it and collecting taxes, although the main duty of a sheriff today is to deal with serious offences brought before his court.

Sheriffs, and indeed all tenants-in-chief, could expect that the king and his court would come to see them from time to time. The government was not fixed in one place. It moved about with the king on his travels throughout the land. In this way the king found out for himself what was going on in all parts of his kingdom. Besides, he could keep himself and his court by living for three or four days on the feasts each lord they visited was expected to provide.

Burghs, Abbeys and Trade

The royal castles were signs that the king was strong. The abbeys, founded by the monks whom David had invited from England and France, showed that he was trying to make Scotland more religious and more civilised. When he made certain villages into royal burghs, he took the first important step to encourage industry and trade. The first Scottish coins, silver pennies, were minted at Roxburgh and Berwick during his reign. Previously, foreign coins had been in use. Though the use of money was not yet common, it made trade with foreign countries easier. Measurements, too, were laid down. An inch (2.54cm) was the length of three good barley grains laid end to end, while an ell, roughly a yard, measured 37 inches (94cm).

By the changes he introduced David I made Scotland a more advanced country, and gave it a pattern of life which was to last for 400 years.

The priest's tithe barn beside the parish church at Foulden, Berwickshire,
which was used for storing the produce people gave him every year

12

Castles in Scotland

Wooden Castles

The first castles in Scotland were all the king's. When he was deciding where to build a castle, he had to ask himself:

1) Is there a good water-supply? (Visitors to Edinburgh Castle can easily find two wells.)

2) Will it be easy to defend?

Usually an outstanding crag or a little hill was a good place, especially at a loop in a river or where two rivers met. Where there were no hills they could make one. They would dig a ditch in a circle and throw all the earth inwards to make a huge mound. This was called a 'motte' (or sometimes mote). The ditch, whether it had water in it or not, was called a 'moat'.

At the Bass of Inverurie in the north-east, Hawick in the Borders and Mote of Urr in Galloway mottes can still be seen. The early towers men built are described well in the following lines:

What a motte and bailey castle looked like

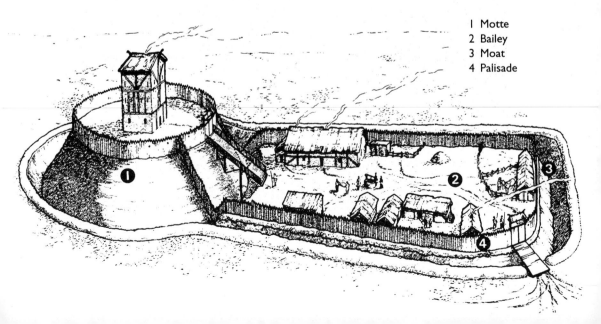

1 Motte
2 Bailey
3 Moat
4 Palisade

A castle entrance with
drawbridge and portcullis

Upon a great dark-coloured rock
He had his house right nobly set
Built all about with wattle-work
Upon the summit was a tower
That was not made of stone and lime.

None of these wooden castles has lasted but the stone castle at Duffus near Elgin is built on the same plan. If you had been visiting this kind of castle during David I's reign, you would cross the water in the moat by the bridge. A sentry opens the strong gate, the only way in. All round the castle is a wall of earth with a palisade, a fence of pointed sticks, on top. You are now in a flat, grassy area, called the 'bailey'. Close to the track you see the byres and stables and pens where all the beasts will be driven tonight for safety. On the left you see servants carrying a side of beef to the kitchen next to the hall. You will eat and be entertained with everyone else tonight, by the big fire in the hall.

You dismount, a man leads your horse away to the stable, while you cross to the motte and clamber up the steps to the tower. You pause and look up. The tower is plain and solid, built of hefty timbers. In times of danger the lord and his family sleep in this tower. The sentry on top has been watching you. He recognises you and waves his hand. You are in a motte and bailey castle.

David I's Norman barons built themselves castles like these, especially in the south-west of Scotland. They were places where people felt safer but there was not much room in a wooden tower, and it was always in danger of being burned down.

Stone Castles

In the late twelfth century kings, and then barons, began to build stone castles. These were stronger and had more room inside. They could be of many different shapes, as you can see if you visit them today. Caerlaverock, near Dumfries, is the only one in Britain to be built in the shape of a triangle on an island in a marsh. It has great round towers at two corners and a strong gateway with a tower on each side of it. Inverlochy Castle in Inverness-shire is square with a round tower at each corner, whereas Rothesay Castle is round and its towers, too, are round.

Defence

Stone castles had thick walls, sometimes nearly three metres in width. The two main buildings were the tower and the hall. As the weakest part of the castle was the doorway, the occupants did everything they could to strengthen it. A drawbridge might be raised up to prevent enemies from reaching it. An iron grill, called a portcullis, dropped down in front of the iron-studded door, would protect it. The top of the tower was reached by a dark spiral staircase, rising and turning clockwise. This meant that a right-handed attacker did not have the freedom to slash with his sword. The sentry on the platform walk on top of the battlements would always be on the lookout for friend or stranger moving towards the stronghold.

As time passed, some castles were built with thicker walls to try to stand against attacks with cannon, but some barons wanted to have strong castles just to make others think they were great men. Even the smaller landowners, the lairds, built towers as fortified places to live in like Smailholm Tower on page 114. These towers, or their ruins, can be seen in many places in Scotland today. They are usually built in the shape of a rectangle, but some have a wing attached, making an L-shape to provide more rooms and more comfort.

The Hall

The hall became the centre of castle life as kings and barons liked to be more comfortable. We know, for instance, that James II did not 'rough it' in Edinburgh Castle. He had a feather mattress and a pillow, and enjoyed wine and salmon. The king's room at Stirling had glass windows. The palace at Falkland had a park and beautiful gardens. The king could play tennis, for example, or have a game of cards or chess, or play his guitar. What he did the barons copied.

Even so, it is doubtful whether we should have considered a castle comfortable. Beautiful tapestries covered some of the stone walls and a rug lay by the fireplace, but most rooms were entered through arches with no doors, and the wind whistled through the long, narrow window-slits, which had to be stuffed with rags in winter. The castle was draughty and dark.

At night, fir splinters or lamps burning fish or animal oil

A lady at her needlework

gave some light, but they made the rooms smoky and smelly. Floors covered in rushes became refuse heaps when scraps fell from the tables. Dogs wandered about. The place smelled of food and filth, animals and people. Although men and women washed their hands at the table, they seldom washed their whole bodies. One writer, in fact, described the Middle Ages in Europe as 'a thousand years without a bath'. In fact, all the rubbish and slops from the castle were tossed into the moat so it was better not to be thrown in there yourself!

In big castles the hall was the place where the king or lord ate in company and in public. He, his family and his guests, sat at a raised table, and were served by squires. The 'salt-fat', or salt container, stood in the centre of the table, and poorer people had to sit 'below the salt' or else at separate tables. The food was placed on the table, and the important people helped themselves first. Dishes were made of silver or wood, and a dagger was handy for cutting meat. For eating, people used spoons and their fingers, as forks had not yet been invented. When the meal was over, people stayed in the hall and drank. They told stories, listened to the minstrel or laughed at the jester. The ladies might go off to spin and weave, make tapestries (woven pictures) or sew napkins and cloths.

The great round tower of Dirleton Castle, east of Edinburgh

The People in Castles

The men in the castle had to defend it and keep up its supply of food. Many animals were killed in November, then cured and hung in the cellars to provide food for the winter, while the granaries were kept full of grain. Pepper and other expensive spices bought from merchants made their food more tasty. The king and the barons enjoyed hunting for deer and wild boar in great areas of wasteland called forests, such as Ettrick Forest near Selkirk. This was a good way of getting fresh meat.

Attached to the larger royal castles, you would meet men with many different jobs: 'bailies' who collected taxes, 'fletchers' who made arrows, 'lorimers' who made spurs and stirrups, porters (door-keepers), as well tailors and cooks, foresters and falconers. Many of them worked in the outbuildings on the bailey. John the cook and William the falconer in time were called John Cook and William Falconer, and this is how many common surnames started.

A lord and his falcon

Visits

Scotland is very rich in castles to visit. Edinburgh Castle, being in the capital, is undoubtedly the most popular and, like it, Stirling Castle is set high on a rock and has for centuries been associated with the royal family. Not far from Edinburgh, Dirleton Castle is interesting for its great round tower, as is Bothwell Castle, which is near Glasgow.

13

From Serf to Freeman

In modern times, we think of the country as being away from the towns and cities where most of the people now live. We talk of going out 'into the country', to be among planted woods and scattered farms. But in Norman times nearly everybody lived in the country – not on farms standing on their own, but in hamlets or little groups of houses called 'touns'. 'Ton' at the end of the name of a place, such as Haddington, means a toun or village.

There were a few towns, not of great importance at first, and these were called 'burghs'. They were really touns which kings or barons or the Church had made into more important places.

Serfs

When David I granted land to barons or the abbeys, he gave them the touns and the people in them too. Every piece of land had its lord, and in David I's reign a law said that if there was any man 'that hes no propir lord', he must find one within 15 days or be fined eight cows – a huge sum. Every toun became subject to a lord or an abbot and the men had to perform certain duties for him in return for their land. Some of them were free but most were serfs. Some were sold, as Turkil Hog and his sons and daughters were to the Prior of Coldingham for three merks of silver (£2). Halden and his brother, William, and their family, on the other hand, were given by the Earl of Dunbar to the Abbey of Kelso. Serfs belonged to their masters, and might have worn iron collars to show what they were and whose men they were. They could not leave the toun or change their jobs. This shows they were not free, but they did have some land, and in those unruly days it was often safer to have a lord's protection.

Farming

The lands of the toun were worked as a whole, the men helping one another in the fields. They farmed to feed themselves and clothe themselves. This is called 'subsistence farming'.

Not all the land was cultivated. Marshy places along the river were too wet to grow anything. The rest of the land was divided into two parts: the patches of infield, nearer to the toun, which always had crops on them, and the outfield, rougher ground further away, which was used mainly for pasture. From time to time, some parts of the outfield were ploughed and planted (but no manure was put on them) until the yield was so low that they were allowed to grow grass again. To grow crops year after year on the same soil, manure is needed, and all the manure from the byres and wood-ash from the cottage fires were carted out to the infield. This land was divided into long strips called 'rigs' or ridges which were ploughed up and down the slope to let the water run off. Each villager's rigs were scattered in different parts of the infield, which ensured that everyone had a share of the good and bad land. Holding land like this is called 'runrig'.

The heavy wooden plough needed from six to 12 oxen yoked to it to pull it. No villager owned so many but each lent one or two to make up the plough-team. At least three men were needed to handle the plough. One man guided it from behind, another put his weight on it to keep the sock down in the furrow, while the third man kept the oxen moving. Turning them was difficult, because they were yoked together in pairs and not harnessed like horses. This probably explains why the rigs were so long and narrow. As much land as possible could then be ploughed with the least number of turns. Other workers would shift big stones and break up hard clods of earth with wooden mallets. Then they would sow seed broadcast by hand, and there was always weeding to be done.

When harvest-time came, mowers stooped to cut the corn with their sickles. Others bound the stalks into bundles and set them up in stooks to dry. Oats were the main crop, for they made oatmeal and oatcakes, while barley was grown for brewing into beer. Peas and beans, cabbages and kale were the main vegetables: turnips and potatoes had not yet been introduced to Britain.

The cattle and sheep of the village grazed on the common pasture or the outfield with the toun-herd ever on the look-out for wolves. About November,

Ploughing a rig

when food for the animals became scarce, the weakest ones were slaughtered. The beef and mutton were salted to provide a stock of food for the family throughout the winter.

In the Highlands and other hill areas it was more difficult to grow crops and most people kept animals. On high land, or where only small patches of ground could be tilled, the spade and the *caschrom* (*see* page 158) took the place of the plough. The caschrom, pressed in with the foot, has been called an early plough, but in using it a man works backwards and turns the soil from right to left, that is, in the opposite way to the plough.

Besides growing crops and keeping animals, the people had many other things to do. There was wood to collect and peat to cut, corn to grind and bread to bake, sheep to shear, yarn to spin and cloth to make (usually from what was called the 'hodden grey', or undyed wool). These were all jobs in which boys and girls could help.

The old dwelling-house might have to be repaired or rebuilt. It was probably built of stone on a wooden framework and roofed with turf or heather. There might be a hole in the roof, not directly over the fire, as a chimney. Inside, all was dark when the door and the window-shutters (used instead of glass) were closed. The cows often sheltered under the same roof.

Furniture was what they made themselves: a table, a bench to sit on, combs, spindles, whorls and a loom for making cloth. The family slept on straw or heather on the earthen floor. Since there was not much cleaning to be done, women spent most of their time making cloth and helping in the fields.

The Coming of Freedom

At Medilham (Midlem) toun,
on the land of the Abbey of Kelso, in 1250

It is just after sunrise on a September morning, and a husbandman [a man with ten hectares of land] and his son are milking their cows.

'It will be a fine morning to start the harvest,' says the father. 'We should manage to cut one rig of oats today, with your mother and the girls to help. Go and sharpen the sickles when you finish with that cow.'

'Yes, father,' replies Adam. 'It will be a change from weeding. The weeds grow as fast as we can cut them.'

But as he goes out of the byre, he hears a voice, the voice of a man on a shaggy pony; it is the steward from the Abbey grange.

'Come on, all you men! All of you to the grange to cut the corn for the Abbey.'

'But we are going to cut our own corn,' mutters Adam.

'Quiet, boy,' his father reproves him. 'We must do as we are told.'

'We shall need you all till the crop is cut,' the steward goes on. 'You husbandmen must do five days' work, and the cottars [cottagers with no land] must come till the work is finished. Come today, and every dry day until you have done the service you owe.'

'Reaping and carrying their corn, shearing their sheep, ploughing their land,' thinks Adam, fingering his iron collar. 'I wish we had only our own work to do.'

By 1290, Adam had his wish. Each of the husbandmen of Medilham held his land, in return for a rent of 11 shillings a year. They had a struggle to pay the rent, for 11 shillings was a lot of money in the Middle Ages, but at least they were now free men.

And, by the time the Scots had won their independence at Bannockburn in 1314, many more of the people were free tenants of the land they farmed.

A ruined farm cottage in Caithness with wooden cruck framework holding up the roof (Crown Copyright: Royal Commission on the Ancient and Historical Monuments of Scotland)

14

The Rise of the Burghs

'The Royal and Ancient Burgh of . . . ' Many a town in Scotland is proud if it can claim to be royal and more ancient than its neighbours. This reminds us that burghs did not simply grow out of small villages. A burgh was created by being given a charter, written and sealed, listing its rights, privileges and duties.

If a burgh gained its charter from the king, it became a royal burgh, if from a lord or from the Church a burgh of barony. The distinction became important in

Edinburgh which grew below the castle compared with the much emptier burgh of Canongate beside Holyrood Abbey, about 1450 (by courtesy of Edinburgh City Libraries)

later times, because only the royal burghs sent representatives to the Convention of Royal Burghs and to Parliament. In David I's reign there were 15 royal burghs: Aberdeen, Berwick, Dunfermline, Edinburgh, Elgin, Forres, Haddington, Linlithgow, Montrose, Peebles, Perth, Renfrew, Roxburgh, Rutherglen and Stirling. Most of these grew up beside a royal castle. They became centres of the king's government and several of them have given their names to shires.

William the Lion was another king who founded many burghs. Burghs of barony which were created by lords include Prestwick and Kirkintilloch, while Glasgow, St Andrews and Canongate (which was then separate from the royal burgh of Edinburgh) are also burghs of barony, but bishops or abbots gave them their charters.

Although a charter was a sign of a burgh's rights, it could not guarantee that it would prosper. Burghs were, above all, places where people traded, and they would only grow if they were in the right places. Ports like Aberdeen, Dunbar and Irvine flourished by fishing, and Dumfries and Berwick relied on the rich lands around them. Berwick exported most of the wool from the Border abbeys. Stirling grew up where an important route crossed the Forth.

Trades and Trade

The burghs were a new stage in the story of how men made a living. The townspeople did not have to meet all their needs by doing everything for themselves. Some would learn a trade, making something to sell, such as shoes; another might do a service for which people were willing to pay, like shoeing horses. The money they earned gave them freedom to buy what they wanted. Merchants lived completely by trading, that is, by buying goods and selling them at a profit. Towns near castles grew because there were people there with money and expensive tastes. Merchants could always sell wines from France, fine woollen cloth from Flanders, honey, onions, figs and spices such as pepper, cinnamon and nutmeg.

The People in the Burghs

Some families had always lived in the burgh. But if serfs escaped from their lords, and held a piece of land in the burgh and stayed free for a year and a day, they, too, could become burgesses. Men from England or Normandy who were skilled in some craft might be allowed to stay, and there were merchants from Flanders, known as Flemings, in places like Berwick and Perth in David I's reign. Later, however, when crafts became organised, members of a trade would not let others with the same trade come in. In the larger towns, especially in the ports, all the merchants joined together in what was called the 'merchant gild' which often gained full control of the affairs of the burgh.

Town Councils and Freedom

At first, each burgess paid rent for his own land to the king's officials, but many burghs saw that they stood to gain if they could run their own affairs. A lump sum, paid to the king each year by the burgh as a whole gave them this right. In 1319, for example, the town of Aberdeen paid the king £213.33. Its burgesses became free men and, equally important, they chose the provost and bailies and 'good men of the better, more discreet and more trustworthy of the burgh' for the town council, with the right to handle the business of the town.

What a Burgh Looked Like

To us the burghs would seem extremely small, more like our present-day villages in size. The townsfolk still relied on the land for much of their food. The town-herd collected their cows early in the morning, drove them out to the common, and brought them back for milking in the late afternoon.

As we approach the burgh, we watch the merchants' servants and others weeding their land on the burgh acres, on our way to the East Port. This is one of the gates in the wall around the town. Inside it we come to a wider area, the market place, and there in the middle is the Mercat Cross. This is where the weekly markets are held and proclamations are read, and where strangers pay their dues on being allowed to trade in the town. Nearby is the little parish church. The market place narrows at one end into the Hie Gate or High Street. It may be the only street. Notice the cobble stones and the open drains. Piles of filth clutter the street; the place smells. Small wonder that plagues are common!

Mostly built of wood, and with thatched roofs, the little houses line the street. Everyone likes to live in the High Street, so, where a piece of land has been split, we may see two narrow houses with their gable ends to the street. Behind the houses some gardens stretch as far as the burgh wall, but with more people coming and wanting houses, new houses are in side streets or up closes at right angles to the High Street. The burgh has the pattern of a fish-bone with the High Street as the main bone.

Round the burgh is a wall of earth with a palisade on top, to keep people safe. They have weapons in their houses to take with them when it is their turn to go on guard after the gates have been closed for the night. This happens at curfew time, when the bell tolls to warn people to damp down their fires. They are always afraid of fire.

Crafts

People learned crafts or trades of all kinds. There were many 'smiths': blacksmiths, goldsmiths and tinsmiths. Some men were websters (weavers), baxters (bakers), fleshers, skinners and glovers. Others might be fletchers, lorimers, saddlers, potters, masons and tailors. New jobs meant new surnames. Many streets and markets, too, take their names from trades, for example, Potterrow, Fleshmarket.

To learn the craft of making shoes, a boy had to become an apprentice for seven years. He worked in his master's workshop in part of the house. He had to be careful to obey his master and his master's wife too, for he lived in their house. Gradually he picked up the secrets of the trade and improved his skill until, at the end of his apprenticeship, he became a tradesman or journeyman (meaning 'paid by the day', from the French *journée*, day).

To become a member of the craft, he had to make his 'masterpiece', a fine pair of shoes. If the deacon of the craft thought this piece of work was good enough, he could set up in business for himself as a master-craftsman. So it was in all the other trades.

Each craft laid down rules for its own members. It limited the number of apprentices a master might employ, fixed wages and prices, set standards of workmanship, and did its best to care for the widows and orphans of its members.

Figure of a souter or shoemaker, an ancient craft in Selkirk

Markets and Fairs

There were no shops. Buying and selling took place on market days each week at stalls in the market place. Some burghs had special markets, which can be detected from street names. The Haymarket and the Lawnmarket (originally Landmarket, where produce of the land was sold) in Edinburgh, and the Coal, Wood and Horse Markets in Kelso are good examples. Fairs did not happen so often. The right to hold a fair was limited to some royal burghs once or twice a year. The luxuries merchants brought from abroad made the countryfolk stand and stare. Making things in the town stopped: this was the time for selling. Acrobats and minstrels came to entertain in what was the highlight of the year.

Many towns still have holidays and 'all the fun of the fair', even where the real reasons for the fair (buying and selling) disappeared long ago; for example, the Glasgow Fair is still held on 7 July, and the Lammas Fair on 1 August in other Scottish towns.

Here are some rules from the charter the king granted to Aberdeen:

1. I forbid any foreign merchant within the sheriffdom of Aberdeen from buying or selling anything except in my burgh of Aberdeen.
2. Foreign merchants will bring their goods to my burgh of Aberdeen and shall there sell them and pay his penny.
3. No one is to keep a tavern in any town in the sheriffdom of Aberdeen unless he is a knight of the town and residing [living] in it.
4. No one residing outside my burgh of Aberdeen shall make or cause to be made any dyed or mixed cloth within the county of Aberdeen except my burgesses of Aberdeen who are in the gild merchant.
5. I forbid any foreigner to buy or sell hides [skins] or wool except within my burgh of Aberdeen.

Kelso markets

15

The Monks of Melrose Abbey

Some of the monks David I brought to Scotland were Cistercians, known as 'White Monks' from the cloaks they wore. They had gone back to the simple life laid down by St Benedict, a life of prayer and work.

Benedict and the Rule

Benedict was the son of a rich Roman noble. When he was at school in Rome in the fifth century AD, he was so horrified by the wicked lives most people led that he left home to live as a hermit in a cave. It was common for holy men to turn their backs on the world and go and live in the wilderness alone, but Benedict was not left on his own. He did not want anyone to follow him but men came, men who wanted to give up their lives to God. He taught them how to live together as a band of equals, calling one another 'brother'. Together they built a great church on the hill called Monte Cassino in Italy.

In the next 500 years, monasteries (houses for monks) were set up all over western Europe. In Scotland, of course, people knew about St Columba and his followers, but they had been monks of a different kind, who lived in separate huts and wandered from place to place as missionaries, preaching to the people.

Benedict drew up the rules of conduct needed by men who were living together all the time. They had two main duties: to worship God (this took them into Church seven times a day) and to work. In addition, they took three vows:

1. Poverty – to give up everything they had;
2. Chastity – never to marry;
3. Obedience – to obey the abbot without question.

An Austin canon at St Andrews

73

Monks in Scotland

David I did most to bring bands of monks from England and France to Scotland. His mother, St Margaret, had invited the first monks to Dunfermline. He gave land to the monks, mainly on the lowlands of the south and east. As time went on, barons also gave some of their lands to the abbeys, which became great landowners with some of the best land in Scotland. Later it was said of David that 'he left the Kirk ower rich and the Crown ower poor'.

There were two main reasons why kings and nobles gave away land like this. The first was that the monks were learned and could do much to improve a backward country. Secondly, people in the Middle Ages were very religious, and they wanted to make sure that when they died they went to Heaven. If they gave lands to an abbey, the monks would pray for their souls.

Melrose Abbey (reconstruction by Alan Sorrell, Crown copyright, courtesy of Historic Scotland)

Monks in Melrose

The first White Monks in Scotland settled at Melrose, on flat land south of the River Tweed. The land was good for growing crops. There were rich meadows for their cows and higher pastures for their sheep. The forest supplied timber for building and fuel. Water from the river drove their corn mill and flushed the great drain which carried waste away from all the buildings. From the slopes of the Eildon hills came a good supply of fresh water, later carried by pipes to the abbey buildings. Good building stone could be quarried nearby.

When they had put up their first simple church, the brothers started to lay out all the other buildings they needed. In course of time, a splendid stone church was built of local stone by bands of masons. They left their marks, cut in the stone on the parts they built. Gradually the brothers were divided into two types:

1. The monks, who took part in all the religious services, wrote and taught and healed.
2. The lay brothers, who did not take full vows, and did most of the heavy work about the abbey and its lands. They lived and slept apart from the monks.

Plan of Melrose Abbey

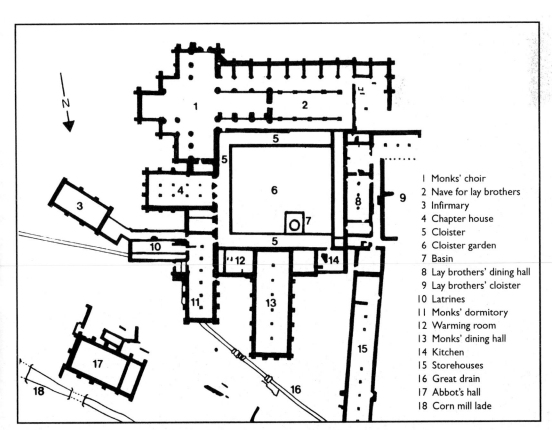

1 Monks' choir
2 Nave for lay brothers
3 Infirmary
4 Chapter house
5 Cloister
6 Cloister garden
7 Basin
8 Lay brothers' dining hall
9 Lay brothers' cloister
10 Latrines
11 Monks' dormitory
12 Warming room
13 Monks' dining hall
14 Kitchen
15 Storehouses
16 Great drain
17 Abbot's hall
18 Corn mill lade

Medieval masons, who built abbeys and castles, at work (figures on display in Stirling Castle)

Imagine visiting Melrose Abbey as it was in the Middle Ages. If we arrive at the abbey after nine in the morning, we shall meet the monks coming from the church after service. This is their fourth service of the day, the first one having been at midnight. They walk slowly, silently, their heads bowed as they make their way along the cloister walk to the chapter house, where they stand quietly, the tiled floor under their sandalled feet, to hear a portion of the rules read to them and to be told what they are to do that day. Two brothers see that the church is ready for the next service. Brother Reginald goes to make more candles from wax for the altar. Brother John sets to work on his accounts, while the others go off to work in the gardens or study in the cloister. There they can only look inwards, for around them on all sides walls of stone shut off their eyes and their minds from the world outside.

In the stables, the horses are harnessed for a nobleman and his followers. There is the nobleman now with his two sons, saying farewell to the abbot after spending the night in the abbot's hall. As we walk towards the cloister, the voices of the boys or novices ring out clearly as they recite their lessons. Passing the monks' dining hall, we see the nobleman's servants loading their horses with food and baggage for the journey north to spend the night at Newbattle Abbey.

As we go out through the abbey gates, the almoner is giving bread to the poor. A heavily-laden cart creaks as axle and solid wheels all turn together, bringing a load of wood for the kitchen fires. And here, wearing a black cloak and a square black cap, comes a bearded monk, an Austin canon, carrying a message from the Abbot of Jedburgh.

Men were all busy, getting ready for the next meal, the next service, the next world. But the abbey was not simply a great church where monks lived; it was a great centre of industry. It imported lime from Kelso, lead for roofs from England and oak from Flanders.

Even people living at some distance from Melrose might have been in contact with it through its lands in Berwickshire on the way to the sea, for example, on the uplands of Selkirkshire, Roxburghshire and Peeblesshire, in the west at Mauchline, Turnberry and Maybole, or in the towns of Perth, Edinburgh and Berwick where the monks had houses.

Monks and Farming

The monks were good farmers. This abbey had nine large farms, called 'granges'. They were really villages, with the hovels of the serfs and their families clustering beside the byres, the corn mill and the brewhouses. Usually one of the lay brothers acted as farm steward. At seed time and harvest all the monks went out to help in the fields. They knew how to grow heavy crops of oats, barley, peas and beans.

They cleared much wasteland and put it under the plough. Alexander II, for example, gave them 'my whole waste of Ettrick'. They set their serfs to improve it and before long it was bringing in a rent of £66 a year.

Several of the monks worked in the gardens and orchards, some kept bees for their honey (there was no sugar in Scotland in the Middle Ages) and some went fishing. The abbey had many of the finest stretches of water in the Tweed, and the monks must have eaten many a meal of trout and salmon.

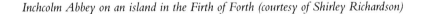

Inchcolm Abbey on an island in the Firth of Forth (courtesy of Shirley Richardson)

They were great breeders of animals. Many oxen were needed for pulling ploughs and carts. Cows and goats were kept for their milk, some of which was made into butter and cheese. The abbey owned hundreds of horses – it is reckoned that at one time it had as many as 1,400. This reminds us how important the horse was in the Middle Ages for carrying men and goods in peace and war. The monks must also have been among the first horse-dealers.

They were most famous, however, for breeding sheep. Sheep, said to total 15,000 in the 1370s, were kept mainly for their soft wool. They were moved up to high pastures in summer and to the lower slopes about September. Roads were so poor that carts could not go far. The fleeces were carried by pack-horses, or on sledges pulled by horses, down the slopes of the Cheviots and Lammermuirs to the abbey, and along the valley to the port of Berwick. There the monks had storehouses, where the wool was kept until ships carried it to Flanders where it was made into fine cloth.

The wool trade made the abbey wealthy. It helped the king and country, too, for the king received customs duties from the wool which was exported, and the sale of wool brought money into the country.

When visiting an old abbey, it is worth trying to imagine the ruined walls raised up into the complete buildings they once were, and to imagine the whole settlement as a place where monks prayed and worked for centuries. Think, too, of the men who built such huge and fine buildings to the glory of God so long ago.

Visits

Melrose Abbey, although in ruins now, is in the care of Historic Scotland and is an excellent abbey to visit and explore. Not far away is Dryburgh Abbey in a beautiful sheltered setting, where Sir Walter Scott lies buried. Abbeys of interest elsewhere in Scotland include Paisley Abbey, now a magnificent parish church; Arbroath Abbey, north-east of Dundee; Dundrennan and Sweetheart Abbeys in Dumfries and Galloway; and Inchcolm Abbey, the best preserved of all, probably because it is on an island in the Firth of Forth (sailings from South Queensferry).

16

The Struggle for Independence under William Wallace

In the end, my friends,
We've nane but the folk; they've nocht [nothing]
To loss [lose] but life and libertie
But gin [if] we've thame, we'va aa. They're Scotland
Nane ither.

Sydney Goodsir Smith, *The Wallace*

The life of the ordinary man working on the land may strike us as humdrum and hopeless, but there was the occasional holiday (holy day) to enjoy, and the hope of a happier life in Heaven. Though he might not notice it in the reign of Alexander III (1249–86), the country was becoming prosperous. People obeyed the king's laws for he kept a firm hold on the land. More burghs were founded, and trade increased, especially through Berwick. There were millions, perhaps 40 million, of silver pennies in use. More and more serfs were gaining their freedom. The Vikings, who had been defeated at Largs in 1263 by storms, disease and Alexander's forces, agreed to hand over the Hebrides to Scotland and to leave the country alone. Scotland was at peace with her southern neighbour. It was an age of peace and prosperity, looked back on later as if it had been a 'golden age'.

When the king's dead body was found on the shore near Kinghorn in 1286 this happy period in Scottish history came suddenly to an end. He left no son to succeed him; the heiress was a little girl, Margaret, the 'Maid of Norway'. When she died in Orkney, Scotland was left without a ruler. The men who claimed the throne might have gathered their men and started to fight each other. Instead, they looked to Edward I of England to choose the next king.

William Wallace, a statue on the way into Edinburgh Castle

Edward had recently conquered the Welsh and built strong castles to keep the peace in Wales, and he dreamed of the whole island being brought under his control. First, he insisted that the claimants recognise him as overlord of Scotland, and then, by the Award of Berwick, he gave the throne to John Balliol who had the best claim.

John Balliol as King

King John ruled like a puppet because Edward pulled the strings. Edward took every chance to show that he was overlord of Scotland, even summoning John to England to pay a wine bill Alexander III owed. When he demanded that the Scots should provide men and money for an English war against France, Edward went too far. Scotsmen had never been forced to fight abroad even for their own king. A council of barons decided to make an alliance with France against their common enemy, Edward I. This Franco-Scottish alliance of 1295, later called the 'Auld Alliance', was to draw both countries together and see Scots and French fighting together against England until the time of Mary, Queen of Scots.

A Scottish raid into England drew the full force of Edward's anger. With a strong army, he captured Berwick and put so many men, women and children in it to the sword that the streets streamed with blood. At Dunbar the Scottish army was defeated, and Balliol soon had to surrender.

Edward's men marched as far north as Elgin. English nobles took charge of the country, and English troops filled the castles. They took away the Stone of Destiny from Scone, where it had been used to install Scottish kings, and put it in the coronation chair in Westminster Abbey. The Holy Rood of St Margaret, said to be part of Christ's Cross, and the bulk of the Scottish records of state, were also taken south. Edward seemed to have Scotland in his power.

The Fight for Freedom

Although most of the nobles had sworn oaths of homage to Edward, few other people welcomed the English soldiers or were willing to pay taxes to the English. The nation's hour of need produced the leaders it required, and people began to fight back in several places. 'But ane nobil young man, callit William Wallace inspyrit by God,' the Scottish writer Androw of Wyntoun tells us, 'tuik pairt with the puir pepill and defendit the realm to the great displeasure and confusion of Inglismen.'

Wallace was not one of the great nobles, but a knight's son from Elderslie in Renfrewshire. He had reason to hate the English. After he had slain an English soldier in a quarrel they killed his wife in Lanark and burned his house. In his fury Wallace led a raid against the English in Lanark and killed Hazelrig, the English sheriff, with his own sword. News of this spread the spirit of rebellion. His band of followers became an army as the common folk flocked to join him. He was a local hero, soon to become a great patriot determined to free his country from the invaders. But a man who is a hero to his fellow-countrymen may be regarded quite differently by his enemies. The monks in a priory just south of the Border wrote this opinion of him in their chronicle:

> A certain bloody man, William Wallace, who before that had been the leading bandit in Scotland . . . induced the poor people to gather to his aid.

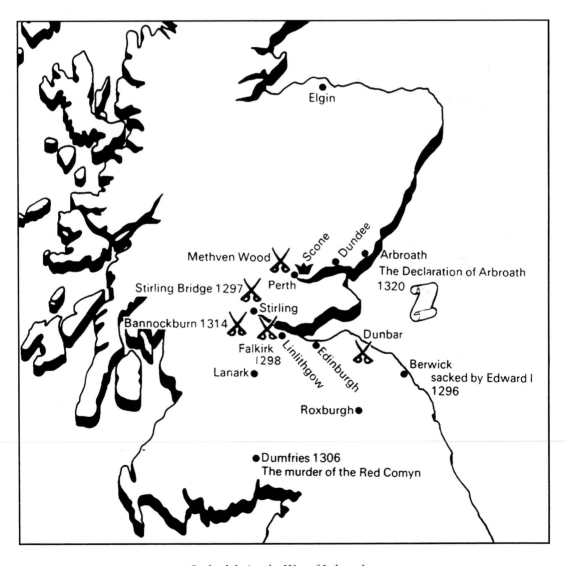

Scotland during the Wars of Independence

Meanwhile a baron's eldest son, Andrew of Moray, was driving the English out of the castles in the north. When Wallace was attacking Dundee in 1297, he heard that an English army was marching north towards Stirling. Andrew of Moray and his men joined him. They made for Stirling and waited in a strong position covering the wooden bridge across the Forth. The bridge was so narrow that men could cross only two or three abreast. When about half of the English army were across, and waiting to re-form their ranks, Wallace sounded his horn for the attack.

The Scots charged with their spears, and captured the end of the bridge. The English who had crossed could not retreat. They perished on the field of battle or in the river. The remainder, who could not cross to help them, were unwilling spectators on the south bank, and then they turned and fled.

Wallace drove the English out of the south-east of the country. Scotland was free, and Wallace and Andrew of Moray were able to show their authority as 'Guardians of Scotland' by inviting the merchants of Lubeck and Hamburg to come back and trade again. But the country was suffering from famine, because of all the fighting. Wallace led an expedition into England, which drove Edward to collect another army and follow the Scots back into Scotland. He caught them and defeated them at Falkirk in 1298. The courage and spears of the Scots were no match for the charges by the English cavalry or the arrows showered down on them. Scotland suffered a serious defeat and Edward had proved himself the 'Hammer of the Scots'.

Having lost the battle, Wallace kept on trying to set the country free. English troops were everywhere, trying to put down local risings. It seemed to Edward that his grip on Scotland would not be tight until Wallace was his prisoner. At last Wallace was tricked by Sir John Menteith, a Scottish knight, who took him prisoner at Robroyston near Glasgow and handed him over to Edward. Wallace was taken to London, tried for treason to a king he did not recognise and condemned to a horrible death. He died for Scotland.

Visits

To find out more about the Wars of Independence, above all visit Stirling. See the Castle guarding the vital river crossing between the Highlands and the Lowlands. View the fifteenth-century bridge, close to the bridge of Wallace's earlier victory, and visit his Monument. Then go on to the Bannockburn Heritage Centre for the story of the battle and the statue of Robert the Bruce.

17

The Struggle for Independence under Robert the Bruce

Ah Freedom is a noble thing!
Freedom makes man to have liking [pleasure];
Freedom all solace [comfort] to man gives;
He lives at ease that freely lives!

John Barbour, *The Brus*

Any hope of Scotland regaining her freedom must have died almost completely when news came that Wallace was dead. English soldiers living in every castle and burgh were signs to the Scottish people that Edward was their lord. The land was bare and food was scarce. But within a year the Scots had a new leader, a man of

Robert the Bruce, King of Scots, the statue at Bannockburn

*Seal of Robert the Bruce
(courtesy of Jennifer Campbell)*

rank who was prepared to give up his English lands to fight for Scotland's freedom. He was descended from the Norman to whom David I had given Annandale, and he had a strong right to be king. His name was Robert the Bruce.

To rid Scotland of the English was difficult enough, but Bruce added to his difficulties. In 1306, at the Grey Friars' Church in Dumfries, he met his rival for the crown, John Comyn (the 'Red Comyn'). They quarrelled, Bruce wounded Comyn with his dagger and, as he rushed out to confess that he had disturbed the peace of a holy place, his friends went in and killed the wounded man. Comyn's men became his deadly foes, and the Church regarded him as a murderer and an enemy of God.

To win support now, he needed to be king. He was made king in secret at Scone; few bishops came because of the ban of the Church on Bruce.

King or Not

Robert the Bruce might now call himself Robert I, King of Scotland, but he was a king hunted in his own country. A defeat by the English in Methven Wood near Perth was followed by another in the west at the hands of the Red Comyn's relatives. He was forced to leave the mainland altogether for a time. When he returned to Ayrshire with a small band of desperate men, he used the tactics of a guerrilla fighter, raiding and ambushing the enemy, but avoiding open battles against larger numbers than his own. He and his men 'lived off the land'. They carried only little bags of oatmeal to make oatcakes; they hunted deer and killed cattle and sheep to feed themselves.

When Edward I, the 'Hammer of the Scots', died in 1307 Bruce's task was easier because his son, Edward II, was not a soldier like his father. This gave Bruce the chance of dealing with his Scottish enemies. He conquered Aberdeenshire, Argyll and Galloway ('the Comyn countries') and had the north of Scotland strongly behind him.

Capturing Castles

At last Bruce could turn on his English foes, the soldiers holding the Scottish castles. Though he took many of the smaller towers quite easily, he did not have the kind of heavy siege-engines needed to capture stone castles by direct attack.

He had to use his eyes to detect weaknesses in their defences, and his wits to trick the enemy. Often his men scaled walls by using rope ladders with hooks, which could be lifted up on the points of their spears to catch the top of a castle wall. They climbed the walls of Perth Castle this way after wading across the moat in winter up to their necks in water; Linlithgow was captured by men hidden under a load of hay; Roxburgh by Sir James Douglas's men wearing dark cloaks and being mistaken for cattle; and Edinburgh Castle by Sir Thomas Randolph's men who daringly climbed the cliffs of the castle rock in the dark.

Edward II's hold on Scotland was slender. Only the castles at Bothwell and Stirling held out for him, and he had to march north at once. He had a splendid army, the largest ever to invade Scotland up to that time. Twenty thousand men raised the dust on the road north to Stirling, their main strength lying in the long column of heavily-armoured knights on horseback. The Scots had only 8,000 men at most and only a few were horsemen and archers. When the Scottish scouts looked out on the enemy and picked out the longbowmen and plumed horsemen, they must have wondered, 'Will this be a defeat like Falkirk, all over again?'

The Battle of Bannockburn, 1314

But Bruce's men were in a good position on the wooded ground of New Park. Protected to the south by the bog, and by the pits which his men had dug near the Bannock Burn as traps for the English horses, they blocked the road to Stirling Castle. Edward must either attack the Scots in the wood, where his cavalry would be hampered, or else take the low road across the marsh between New Park and the Forth. On the afternoon of 23 June, the English cavalry tried a direct attack on the Scots in the wood, but some floundered in the pits and the rest withdrew. The English knight, De Bohun, charged the Scottish king but Bruce felled him at the cost of his good battle-axe.

The sacred box, or reliquary, which once held relics of St Columba (courtesy of the Trustees of the National Museums of Scotland)

Edward's army crossed the Bannock Burn and camped for the night. In one sense, the water protected them; in another sense, they were in a trap. When the sun came up, columns of Scottish spearmen advanced boldly down the slope, then stopped and knelt in prayer. A sacred box of the relics of St Columba was held up before them. They believed it would help them to win.

'See,' said Edward, 'they kneel to ask for mercy.'

'Yes, sire, but not from you,' said a knight near him. 'It is God's mercy that they seek. These men will conquer or die.'

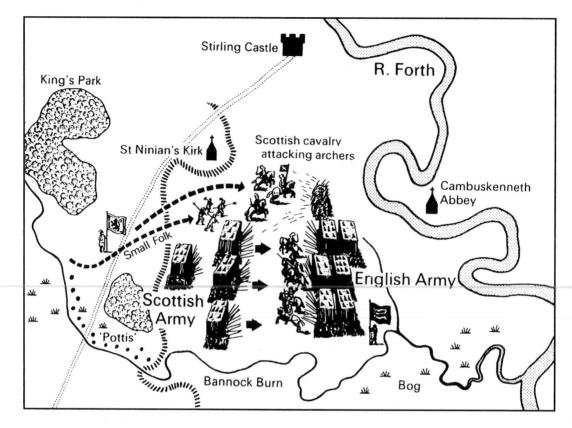

Plan of the Battle of Bannockburn

Edward could not believe it. Here came Scottish foot-soldiers in columns, their spears thrust out like the prickles of a hedgehog, daring to attack English knights and bowmen. A counter-attack by the English cavalry crumbled before the Scottish spears; a word from Bruce and his horsemen routed the English archers. This certainly would not be the battle of Falkirk over again. But the battle was not yet won. The English had far more men and equipment, but they had no room to spread out on a wide front. The fighting was desperate, hand-to-hand. You could hear the clang of sword on armour, the splintering of wood, the mad gallop of riderless horses, the shouting, the moans of dying men. The battle was confused, but the English were trapped with water at their backs.

Probably by Bruce's orders, the 'small folk', the armed farmers and camp-followers, left their shelter in the valley and came to the field of battle.

'On them,' they shouted. 'On them! They fail!' Their arrival encouraged the Scots; they seemed like a fresh army to the English who broke and fled. The Forth swallowed many an English knight. An early writer tells us that, 'Bannockburn was so full of bodies that on top of drowned horses and men, men could pass over it dryshod [without getting their feet wet].'

The Battle of Bannockburn, on 24 June 1314, was Scotland's greatest victory. Much booty was taken, and the English surrendered Stirling Castle. For several years raids into the north of England were made until independence was won and the English signed the Treaty of Northampton in 1328. Scotland was a free and separate kingdom.

What the Scots had been fighting for is best described in the *Declaration of Arbroath*. Written in 1320, this document was sent to the Pope, asking him to recognise Robert I as king of an independent Scotland:

> For so long as one hundred men remain alive, we shall never under any conditions submit to the domination of the English. It is not for glory or riches or honour that we fight, but only for liberty, which no good man will consent to lose but with his life.

Arbroath Abbey where the Declaration was signed in 1320 and where the Stone of Scone (or Destiny), taken from Westminster Abbey, was placed in 1950

Bruce's Heart

Bruce had saved Scotland and made its people a nation. But could he save his own soul? As long as the ban of the Church was on him, he could not be buried as a Christian and believed he had no prospect of reaching Heaven. At length, worn down by his labours and very ill, he heard the good news that the Pope recognised him as king and as a faithful member of the Church. He was never able to go on a crusade as he had wished, but he made Sir James Douglas, 'the good Sir James', promise to carry his heart, enclosed in a casket, to the Holy Land after his death.

For the past 200 years, Christian knights from many nations had fought in the Crusades or 'Wars of the Cross', to free Palestine from the Mohammedan Turks who had conquered it. Few Scots had gone there to fight, because they were needed to defend their own country against England. Sir James Douglas and his companions, however, set out and fought against the Mohammedans in Spain. There, in the thick of the battle, Douglas and his followers were killed. Bruce's heart was returned safely to Scotland and placed in Melrose Abbey.

Rulers after David I

Ruler	Description
Malcolm IV, 1153–65	Grandson of David I, unmarried, called 'the Maiden'
William I, 1165–1214	Malcolm's brother, later called 'the Lion'
Alexander II, 1214–49	William's son, established Tweed–Cheviots boundary with England
Alexander III, 1249–86	Alexander II's son, married daughter of Henry III of England: all their children died before him
Margaret, 1286–90	The 'Maid of Norway', Alexander III's grand-daughter, a child in Norway who died, aged eight, in Orkney
John I, 1292–96	John Balliol, deposed by Edward I
Robert I, 1306–29	Robert the Bruce, victor at Bannockburn

18

The Later Middle Ages

This is my country,
The land that begat me.
These windy spaces
Are surely my own,
And those who here toil
In the sweat of their faces
Are flesh of my flesh
And bone of my bone.

Sir Alexander Gray: *Scotland*

The Wars of Independence were Scotland's moment of glory when the people felt they had become a nation. But the price of victory was heavy. They had tried their hardest to win against a great and wealthy neighbour, and most of the battles had been fought on Scottish soil. People and beasts, burghs and touns, castles and kirks, had all suffered heavily, and the men who fought for Bruce had to rebuild what had been knocked down.

We do not know how many people were living in Scotland then. Probably there were half a million or more in Bruce's time – not much higher than the population of Edinburgh at the end of the twentieth century. Famine and fighting always kept the numbers down, but in 1349–50 a great plague struck the country. This was the Black Death, which had already killed millions in Europe. It spread from England into Scotland, where people called it 'the Foul Death of the English'. Many people in Scotland died: we do not know the number but it may have been as many as one person out of every four.

More Wars

After the Wars of Independence the country needed a period of peace under a strong king. But when Robert the Bruce died, he was succeeded by a boy, David II. England under Edward III was still the 'Auld Enemy', and refused to recognise David II as king, instead making Edward Balliol, John's son, king of Scotland.

English troops marched north in 1333 in the hope of capturing Berwick, Scotland's busiest seaport. Edward's archers slaughtered the Scottish army at the battle of Halidon Hill, and then took Berwick and held it for a time. Soon Scotland

What a fourteenth century knight, Bricius MacKinnon, looked like, from the slab on his grave in Iona (Crown Copyright: Royal Commission on the Ancient and Historical Monuments of Scotland)

suffered more burning and killing. Even towns in the north such as Elgin and Aberdeen were burned, and some of the castles which Bruce's men had destroyed were built up again and filled with English troops.

In the north, Andrew of Moray, whose father had shared the victory at Stirling Bridge with William Wallace, defeated Edward Balliol's supporters near Ballater in 1335. Gradually he freed most of Scotland for David II.

In the south 'Black Agnes', Countess of March, held out in Dunbar Castle for months against an English siege. Food brought in by boat at night from the Bass Rock saved the defenders from starving. Mockingly she sent some to the English commander and in disgust he gave up trying to capture the castle.

Fortunately for Scotland, Edward needed most of his soldiers elsewhere. In 1337 he attacked France, in what was to become the 'Hundred Years War'. By the Auld Alliance, the Scots were still expected to make raids on the north of England. In one raid south of the Tyne they were defeated at Neville's Cross (1346). Wounded in the face by an arrow, David II was taken prisoner. His ransom cost £66,000, a crippling sum for a poor country.

Robert II became king in 1371. His claim to the throne was sound, for he was the son of Walter the Steward and Marjory Bruce, the eldest daughter of Robert I. At the age of 55 he became the first of the Stewart line of kings. He tried to remain at peace with England, but in 1385 over 1,000 French knights arrived in Scotland to raid the English. The attack failed, and the enemy came north and burned Edinburgh and the abbeys of Melrose and Dryburgh.

In 1388 the Earl of Douglas advanced into the lands of Henry Percy in the north of England. Percy attacked Douglas at Otterburn. The armies fought on fiercely by moonlight, with axe and spear, sword and dagger. Three times wounded, Douglas fell, but the English did not know that the Scottish leader was dying. The Scots attacked, shouting 'Douglas! Douglas!' and drove the English from the field. Douglas died, but he had won as he had dreamed he would, according to the old ballad, *The Battle of Otterbourne*:

I saw a dead man win a fight,
And I think that man was I.

Kings and Barons

KINGS OF SCOTLAND 1329–1488

David II	1329–71
Robert II	1371–90
Robert III	1390–1406
James I	1406–37
James II	1437–60
James III	1460–88

Alnwick Castle in Northumberland, home of the Percy family, with statues of men on the ramparts to frighten the Scots

After the Wars of Independence Robert I took lands away from the barons who had fought against him and gave them to men who had served him well. This made some families very powerful, but there was no danger in this as long as he was king. After Robert I, however, Scotland was unfortunate in her kings. David II was only five when he became king and was later held prisoner in England for 11 years; Robert II, the first of the Stewarts, was too old; his son Robert III was a kind man, but weak; then James I was held prisoner in England for 18 years. For almost a century (1329–1424) no king had the money, the men or the willpower to rule Scotland firmly from the centre.

Under a weak or absent king, the heads of big landed families ruled in their own areas as if *they* were kings. Their relatives supported them and lower families in the area found it wise to join them as well. It gave them protection but it added to the number of armed men a great lord could command. Some lords, especially the Earls of Douglas, became very powerful. Other important families were the Crawfords, the Gordons, the Ogilvies, the Lindsays, the Hamiltons, the Homes and, later in the south-west, the Kennedys:

> Frae Wigton to the toon o' Ayr
> Port Patrick to the Cruives o' Cree,
> Nae man wad think to bide there
> Unless he coort wi' Kennedy.

It was very difficult to make people take heed of laws in the Highlands. As soon as Robert III, a gentle, crippled old man, became king in 1390, his own brother Alexander, known as the 'Wolf of Badenoch', started to cause trouble in the north. With a band of 'wild, wikkit hielandmen', he raided the lands of the Bishop of Moray and burned down his cathedral at Elgin. In other places, clan fights took place often and the king could not stop them. At a clan fight in Perth, Robert III was a helpless spectator as 30 champions from each of the two clans Chattan and Kay fought each other with axe, sword and dagger until nearly all were slain.

Such troubled times drove the king to send his son, James, to France for safety, but the boy might have been safer at home. His ship was captured by the English, and he was their prisoner for 18 years.

When his father died, regents ruled in young James's place. The Lord of the Isles was the master of all the lands in the west from Kintyre in Argyll to the Isle of Lewis in the north, and he made treaties with England as if he were a king. In 1411, Donald, the second Lord of the Isles, led an army of Highlanders towards Aberdeen. He claimed that the earldom of Ross in the north was his, and was ready to fight for it. At Harlaw his army was driven off by spearmen from Buchan and Angus under the Earl of Mar, who were supported by burgesses from Aberdeen. Many were killed on both sides:

> And Hieland and Lowland may mournful be
> For the sair field of Harlaw.

James I (detail from a painting by an unknown artist.
Courtesy of the Scottish National Portrait Gallery)

A battle like this shows how much Scotland needed a king who could stop one baron, or one group of men, from fighting another.

Kings Who Tried Hard, One Who Did Not

JAMES I

When James I returned from England in 1424, he showed that he was a strong king. He was manly and intelligent, and said he would make Scotland so law-abiding that the key would be enough 'to keep the castle and the bracken-bush the cow.' He called parliaments to help him (from the French word *parler*, meaning 'to speak'), to which representatives of the Church and the burghs came along with the barons. Parliament's job was to agree to taxes and to make laws. For example, Parliament ordered every man to have the proper weapons for a man of his rank

James II and the cannon which killed him on a monument carved in the 1790s beside Dryburgh Abbey

and to practise with the bow and arrow in case he was called to fight for the king. Barons were ordered not to have too many armed followers when they rode about the country, and were not to make private wars on one another.

James acted swiftly against the barons and chiefs, who had not been used to having to obey a strong king. He captured his cousin, the Duke of Albany, who had been regent when James was in England, and had him executed at Stirling. In 1428 James ordered the Highland chiefs to meet him in Inverness. He threw over 40 of them in prison, including the Lord of the Isles, and put the most dangerous to death. Measures like these did not make Highlanders feel that James was a good king.

A few nobles plotted to kill him when he was staying at the Blackfriars in Perth in 1437. He was warned that he was in danger but he paid no attention. One evening when he was talking with the queen and her ladies, there was a clink of weapons outside. James was unarmed and it was discovered that the door could not be closed. In a much later story we are told that Katherine Douglas, one of the queen's attendants, used her arm to bar the door while the king escaped through the floorboards to the drains below. When the armed men burst in, the king was nowhere to be found and they departed. Something, probably a noise, called them back. They noticed the loose boards and plunged down. James was trapped and murdered.

JAMES II

James II was crowned at Holyrood when he was only six. The king's guardians, Crichton and Livingston, were frightened of what the other barons would do. They invited the young Earl of Douglas, the most powerful of them, and his brother to come to Edinburgh to visit the king. They came and were entertained to dinner. Then the head of a black bull was placed on the table: it was a sign of death. Young James protested but his guests were hustled off and put to death.

When James II became a man, he tried to be a strong king like his father. He was guided by Bishop Kennedy of St Andrews. Parliament supported him and so did the Church but he knew that he would not be the real king until he proved that he was stronger than the Douglas family. When he discovered that the new Earl of Douglas had made an agreement to join with other earls, he ordered him to come to Stirling Castle, promising that no harm would come to him. James told him bluntly that this league of barons must be broken up at once. Douglas defied him, and James drew his dagger and stabbed him. This action by the king stung the Douglases into rebellion. On Kennedy's advice, James was careful to take on Douglas's allies one at a time. Then, attacking them with heavy cannon, he knocked down their castles and took back all their lands for himself. The power of the Douglases was at an end. This king had shown that he was mightier than any baron.

James II was one of the first to use cannon to blast holes in the castles of barons who would not obey him, and he was the king who brought the great cannon called Mons Meg from Belgium, now in Edinburgh Castle. His reign ended in tragedy, however, when he was using cannon to try to win back Roxburgh Castle from the English. He was watching one of them being fired in 1460, when it blew up and killed him.

JAMES III

Once again the new king was only a boy. In 1469 he married Margaret, daughter of the king of Denmark, who was to bring him a large sum of money as her dowry. When this dowry was not paid, Orkney and Shetland passed to the Scottish crown instead.

James III was not a man of action like his father and grandfather. He trusted no one, not even his own brothers. He was either too lazy or too frightened to govern and did not trouble to travel about the country to see that justice was done. He was not hard enough on the nobles who kept quarrelling with one another. Later they turned against him and would not even fight for him against the English. When he was assembling men to defend the port of Berwick against English invaders, his nobles captured him at Lauder and held him prisoner for a time in Edinburgh. No Scottish army marched to save Berwick, which has been an English town ever since.

Powerful nobles rose against the king again in 1488. They had his 15-year-old son, James, with them calling himself 'Prince of Scotland', and said they fought in his name. Father and son and their two armies faced each other in battle at Sauchieburn near Stirling. Thrown from his horse, James III was carried to a corn mill. Thinking he was going to die, he asked for a priest. He was stabbed there by a dagger in an unknown hand.

19

The Age of Discovery

It is impossible to say exactly when a boy becomes a youth or when a youth becomes a man. In the same way, we know that one age in history differs from the age before it, but we cannot say exactly when the new age begins.

The Middle Ages, the period we have been studying, was the time when the Pope was recognised as God's representative on earth and every Christian looked to him for guidance. Inside each country, on the other hand, a man's position depended on the land he held. Thus, the priest in his church and the lord in his castle were the two great authorities whom everyone believed and obeyed. Churchmen were the only educated men, and people were brought up to believe what they said. 'What do the scholars say?' people asked. 'These things we must learn and believe.'

In the fourteenth and fifteenth centuries, people's ideas began to change. They were no longer satisfied with what somebody told them to believe. They began to ask questions, not about the next world but about the world around them. They became curious about its shape and its size, and about the stars and the planets. They also wanted to experiment, to prove things for themselves. To find the truth became a quest: it was the real way to learn. This new age was called the 'Renaissance', meaning the rebirth of enthusiasm for learning.

The Renaissance

The Renaissance began in Italy, in cities like Florence and Venice where merchants came into contact with the ideas of foreign lands in the course of trade. The people in Italy could see around them ruins that reminded them that ancient Rome had been a great civilisation. Perhaps thinkers in early Greece and Rome had known more about the world than they did. Gradually manuscripts written in Greek were brought to Italy where they were eagerly studied. This trickle of documents became a flood when the Turks captured Constantinople in 1453 and Greek scholars living there fled to the West. Those who settled in Italy brought their valuable manuscripts with them.

New discoveries were made in science. As early as the thirteenth century, Roger Bacon knew about gunpowder, which, when used in pistols and cannon, was to blast the armoured knight and the castle from the thoughts of military men.

A king who had artillery at his command could keep his barons in order. Copernicus, a Polish astronomer, discovered that the earth was not fixed but moved round the sun. Galileo, the Italian scientist, first used the telescope to support the ideas of Copernicus. In another experiment, he dropped stones of different sizes from the top of the leaning tower of Pisa, and proved that they fell at the same rate even though some were heavy and some were light. Leonardo da Vinci, artist, architect, town-planner, sculptor and engineer foresaw the aeroplane and the 'covered chariot' (the tank).

In the Middle Ages, students spoke Latin and travelled about Europe to study under great teachers in the universities. Now many were attracted to Italy to study Greek. When they returned home to Germany, France, the Netherlands and Britain, they carried their craze for learning with them.

In Germany, the printing press was invented by John Gutenberg, and in 1476 William Caxton set up his press in England. Following the discovery by the Arabs of a cheap way of making paper, it became possible to produce books in large numbers. By the year 1500, there were nine million printed books in Europe, compared with about 100,000 written by hand in the whole of the Middle Ages. More people learned to read and write and so to find things out for themselves.

Other men felt the urge to create. Some were great artists, such as Leonardo da Vinci, who painted the 'Mona Lisa'. Some were architects who went back to the Greeks for inspiration. They tried to make their buildings in proportion, so that their breadth and height were 'just right'. They gave up building arches and built doorways and windows with lintels over them, as we do today; and some of their new buildings had columns and domes. St Peter's Church in Rome, and St Paul's Cathedral in London which Sir Christopher Wren rebuilt in the seventeenth century, have many of these new features.

Voyages of Discovery

People wanted to find out about other lands. The world they knew in the Middle Ages was small. It consisted of Europe and the lands round the Mediterranean, to which Arab traders brought the wealth of the East from India, China and the Indies, which people called the Spice Islands. It was possible to explore once sailors had the compass to guide them.

Prince Henry of Portugal, known as 'the Navigator', encouraged his sea-captains to sail farther and farther south along the coast of Africa. Following them, Bartholomew Diaz reached the Cape of Good Hope in 1488 and then Vasco da Gama sailed round the Cape and crossed the Indian Ocean, and in 1498 he arrived in India. This was to be the route sailors took to the East until the Suez Canal was opened in 1869.

But if the world is round, why not reach India by sailing west? In 1492 Christopher Columbus, a sailor from Genoa, sailed west with three ships Isabella, the Queen of Spain had given him. Weeks on the open sea terrified his men but Columbus kept them going. At last they reached land, one of a group of islands which included Cuba and Haiti. Columbus thought they were the Spice Islands and called them Indies. On later voyages he touched the mainland. This was not Asia, as he had hoped, but South America.

Other captains sailed west. John Cabot found Newfoundland and claimed it for England; Amerigo Vespucci, whose name was given to America, explored the coast of South America and Balboa crossed the land of Panama and first gazed on another great sea, the Pacific Ocean, to the west.

But they had not yet reached India by sailing west.

In 1519 Ferdinand Magellan set off from Spain with five ships to try to solve the problem. Trying to sail round South America, they made their way through the strait which is now named after their leader, and entered the Pacific Ocean. They sailed for months, running out of food with never a sight of land. Then they reached the Philippines where Magellan died fighting the natives. His men sailed on, to the East Indies, where they loaded up with food and spices. Then they crossed the Indian Ocean and went on round the Cape of Good Hope, until just one leaking ship and 18 men got back to Spain. They had sailed right round the world.

Voyages of Discovery

James IV by Daniel Mytens (in the collection of the Stirlings of Keir)

They were exciting times, as exciting as our own. Adventurers returned with gold and silver, black men and strange stories. They had conquered the oceans as we have conquered the air and space. A new continent, America, had appeared over the western seas, and the countries facing the Atlantic (Spain, Portugal, France and England) were well placed to become wealthy by trade.

Scotland under James IV (1488–1513)

Let us consider Scotland's position in this new age. The country produced no outstanding artists, scientists or explorers. It stood on the fringe of the great changes in Europe. At the court, however, the king was determined that his country should not be out-of-date. James IV was a great all-rounder, a good athlete and horseman, a keen scientist and surgeon and it was said that he knew Latin and Gaelic and five foreign languages.

He tried to make all his people obey him. He took away the title of Lord of the Isles from Clan Donald in 1493, and five times in the next ten years went into their lands to quell them. Keen to learn what was going on in his kingdom, James kept making tours to see things for himself, and to make sure that justice was being done.

Scotland already had two universities, St Andrews (1413) and Glasgow (1451), and James IV founded the third at Aberdeen in 1495 to produce lawyers and, for the first time in Britain, to train doctors as well. Then he recognised the craft of surgery in Edinburgh and allowed no one to carry out operations unless he had been properly trained. In 1496 he ordered barons and freeholders to send their eldest sons to grammar schools at the age of eight or nine, until they had 'perfect Latin and understanding of the laws'. For the first time, boys who were not going to be churchmen were encouraged to be educated.

The printing of books began in 1508, much later than in other countries. In their shop in Edinburgh, Walter Chapman and Andrew Millar published their first volume. It included poems by William Dunbar, who wrote *The Thistle and the Rose* to celebrate the wedding of James to Margaret Tudor of England. Dunbar, a

King's College, Aberdeen, the university James IV founded in 1495

wandering scholar who became one of the king's clerks, was a great poet. He wrote, not in Latin, but in the language of his own people. Gavin Douglas translated the works of Latin poets like Virgil and Horace into 'the braid Scots'. A Dunfermline schoolmaster, Robert Henryson, told fascinating stories about animals in his *Moral Fables*. What do you think of his description of the worried little mouse in these lines?

> Ane lytill mous come till ane rever [river] syde;
> Scho [she] micht not waid, hir schankis [legs] were sa short,
> Scho culd not swym, scho had na hors to ryde;
> Of verray force behovit [of necessity forced] her to byde,
> And to and fra besyde the Rever deip
> Scho ran, cryand with mony pietuous [pitiful] peip.

James IV was curious about science and bought books and chemicals, and carried out experiments of his own. He was taken in by John Damian, a foreigner, and spent a lot of money on him. Damian claimed that he could turn other metals into gold, and even tried to become the first man to fly. Wearing wings made of feathers, he leapt from the walls of Stirling Castle. According to Dunbar, who made fun of Damian's efforts:

> And in the myre [mud], up till the een [eyes],
> Among the glaur did glyde

When English pirates interfered with Scottish trading vessels in the Firth of Forth, Sir Andrew Wood of Largo in Fife went out with two ships, the *Flower* and the *Yellow Carvel*, to fight them. After a desperate battle, he captured the five English ships.

To build real fighting ships, James brought ship-builders over from France and the Netherlands. In the royal dockyard at Newhaven near Leith they built stout ships, including the *Great Michael*, the biggest ship of her day. To build her, we are told, men 'cut all the woods of Fife, except Falkland Wood, in addition to all the timber that was brought out of Norway'. Measuring 75 metres from stem to stern, she was armed with more than 300 guns and it took 300 men to sail her. She made Scotland a power to be reckoned with at sea.

The Battle of Flodden

While English troops were fighting against the French in 1513, James declared war on Henry VIII of England. Men from all over Scotland joined him and he advanced over the Border. His big guns won him Wark and Norham castles.

Then he took up such a strong position on Flodden Hill that the Earl of Surrey, the English commander, dared not attack him. But Surrey led his men round the side of the Scottish army and placed them between the Scots and their road back to Scotland. Under cover of smoke the Scots turned to face them. The English artillery out-gunned the Scots, and its accurate fire tore great gaps in the Scottish ranks. The battle was fought on foot, but the Scots, armed with four-and-a-half-metre pikes, lost formation as they crossed the rough ground. These awkward weapons were useless at close quarters against the English 'halberds' or bills, which were much shorter and could be used both as spears and battleaxes. James, who led the charge himself, had his pike shattered, and was killed only a pike's length from the Earl of Surrey. In the hand-to-hand battle that followed, the Scots could not reach the English bill-men with their swords. The Scots 'could not resist the bills that lighted so thick and so sore upon them', and thousands were killed.

It was more a massacre than a battle. Though the Scots had as many men and had more guns and food-supplies, they were a feudal host compared with this English army of professional soldiers, disciplined and armed with a weapon to which the Scots had no answer. Scotland was not as modern as it had thought.

Fighting at close quarters at Flodden, the bill was the handier weapon

20

Changes in Religion in Scotland, England and Europe

In most towns in Scotland you will find at least two places of worship, one Church of Scotland and one Roman Catholic, because nowadays not all Christians agree on what they believe or how they should worship. They are free to choose the church they want to attend. Until the sixteenth century, however, everyone in western Europe was a member of the same church, the Roman Catholic Church, headed by the Pope in Rome. Every town and parish had its church and everybody went to it. Why and how, then, did people become members of different Churches?

The State of the Church in Scotland

Over the years, kings and nobles had given a lot of land to the Church and by the mid-sixteenth century the Church's income had risen to £400,000 a year. Compare this with the income of the king at that time – he had never had more than £45,000 a year. It was no surprise that the king, and bishops and archbishops too, wanted to get some of the Church's great wealth for themselves. James IV, for example, made his own son Archbishop of St Andrews when he was only eleven years old, so that he could have the income which came from this high position. Nobles asked the king to make their clerical relatives abbots or sometimes guardians of abbeys so that they could share in the money that flowed into them. Men like these did not always help the Church to do its work.

When abbeys became rich, some men wanted to be monks simply because it had become a comfortable life. In 1534, for example, it was found that every monk in Melrose Abbey had a private garden and was receiving money of his own to spend on clothes – a far cry from the vow of poverty each monk would have taken.

By 1560, 17 out of every 20 parish churches in Scotland had been taken over by some abbey or cathedral. These great churches collected the tithes – the tenth part the people gave each year from their crops and young animals – and they spent them somewhere else. They sent vicars to take the place of the priests, but these men were paid so little that they would not do anything for people until they were paid. This happened, for example, when someone in a family died, as Sir David

Lindsay tells us:

> Our vicar took the best cow by the head
> Within an hour, when my father was deid.
> And when the vicar heard tell how that my mother
> Was deid, frae hand he took frae me another.

The usual church service was in Latin. The vicars could recite it but many of them did not understand it. The Archbishop of St Andrews tried to improve things by issuing the clergy with a new book in Scots to instruct the people. He ordered them to practice reading it so that they would not stammer when they read in church and be laughed at by the congregation. He also told bishops and priests to preach at least four times a year.

Printing, too, played its part. William Tyndale's translation of the Bible into English was published, and traders brought copies back with them to Scotland. When people, and especially scholars, studied the Gospel they found fault with some things that the priests were teaching.

The Reformation in Europe

Martin Luther, a German professor, was the first to raise his voice in anger. Hearing that a friar was selling 'pardons' for sins, even for the sins of relatives long dead, he could not keep quiet. He felt that a man would only be forgiven if he were truly sorry for his sin. Here he saw his countrymen paying for what he thought were worthless promises. Hard-earned German money was going to Rome to help to build the magnificent Church of St Peter. He made a list of 95 arguments against these pardons, and nailed them to the church door in Wittenberg in 1517.

Luther began to attack other faults in the Church and the Pope himself. The Pope drove him out of the Church, and the Emperor made him an outlaw. Luther burned the Pope's letter in the market place, but he then had to go into hiding. He translated the Bible into German. The hymn he wrote, *A Safe Stronghold our God is Still*, had half Germany singing. A law was passed which would have crushed the churches which Luther's followers were setting up but many of the German princes protested. They were given the name Protestants.

Luther had tried to point out a fault in the Church, but the Pope would not correct it. The movement Luther started, called the 'Reformation', split the Church and divided people into Catholics and Protestants.

The Catholic Church then began to put its own house in order. Its chief reformer was a Spanish soldier, Ignatius Loyola. After being severely wounded in battle, he decided to become a soldier for Christ. He formed a new order, the Society of Jesus, whose members were called 'Jesuits'. They started schools, and trained priests who went into every land to give Catholic answers to the new ideas.

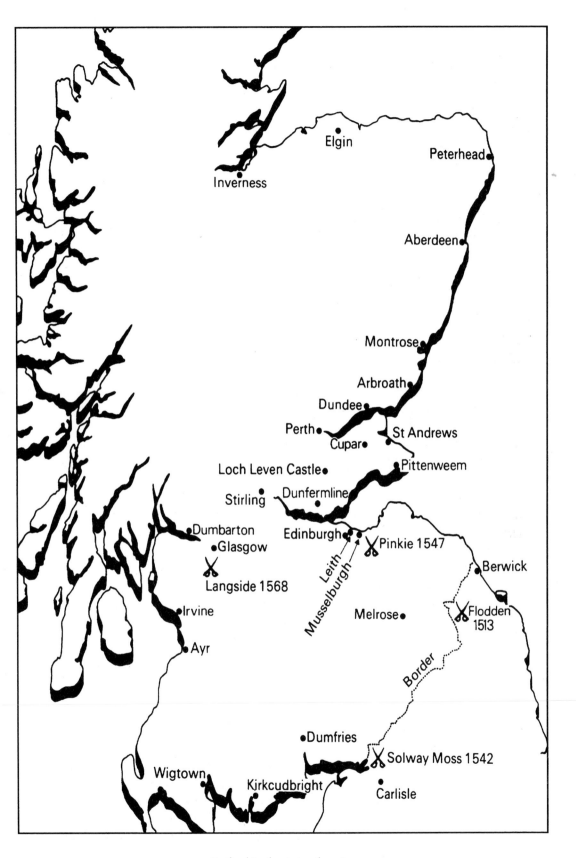

Scotland in the sixteenth century

TOP: *'P. H.', the initials of Patrick Hamilton, mark the place where he was burned in St Andrews*

BOTTOM: *George Wishart (detail from a painting by an unknown artist. Courtesy of the Scottish National Portrait Gallery)*

Scotland and England

Patrick Hamilton was one of the Scottish students at universities in Europe and came back from Germany filled with Luther's ideas. His preaching led to his being burned at the stake in St Andrews. Burning him, however, did not make people forget him, and it was said, 'the reek [smoke] of master Patrick Hamilton infected as many as it blew upon'.

Scotland's king, James V, married a Frenchwoman, Mary of Guise in 1538. This bound him to support both the Auld Alliance with France, and the Church of Rome. In England, on the other hand, King Henry VIII, wishing to rid himself of his wife, quarrelled with the Pope. He got Parliament to make him head of the Church in England. He closed all the abbeys, drove out the monks and took their lands. To stop Scotland helping France, Henry's army came north and routed the Scots at Solway Moss in 1542. James died heart-broken, leaving a new-born girl to become the beautiful but unfortunate Mary, Queen of Scots.

Henry suggested that his son, Edward, and the child, Mary, should marry when they were old enough. This would have broken off Scotland's alliance with France and united Scotland and England. When the Scots refused, Henry sent his army north under the Earl of Hertford. They captured Edinburgh and set it on fire. It burned for four days. The English boasted that in all they burned or cast down 192 towns, towers, churches and farmsteads, and drove 10,000 cattle, 12,000 sheep and 1,000 horses over the Border. The next year, 1545, Hertford was back, burning the grain harvest and the Border abbeys as well. He returned two years later and smashed another Scottish army at Pinkie, near Musselburgh.

These raids, called the 'Rough Wooing', did not win the hearts of the Scots. Instead, Mary was sent to France to be brought up in safety. But it did help to destroy the old Church. This was the time when people learned more about the Word of God as Bibles in English were brought into seaports and over the Border. The Scottish nobles were interested to learn how people like them in England had become rich when lands taken from the abbeys passed into their hands.

However, these were dangerous times for Protestant preachers, but George Wishart was one who still took the risk. He was arrested, condemned for preaching against the Catholic Church and burned in St Andrews. Then the Catholic leader, Cardinal Beaton, was killed in revenge. The men who killed him held out in St Andrews Castle. John Knox joined them but they were captured after a long siege in 1547 and sent to France as prisoners. After 19 months rowing as a galley-slave, John Knox became a minister in the free city of Geneva. He came under the spell of John Calvin, the French Protestant minister who ruled the city. He learned to put his faith in the people rather than in princes and bishops. He saw that Calvin's followers preferred sermons to ceremonies, and worshipped in a church which was plain and undecorated.

In 1559 John Knox came back to Scotland where few Protestants were still preaching.

Visits

Visit the Castle Visitor Centre in St Andrews for imaginative scenes of the events during the Reformation. This historic town also holds Scotland's oldest university, and has many traces of the medieval burgh, as well as, of course, preserving centuries of golfing history.

Melrose Abbey Church now in ruins, burned by the English in the 'Rough Wooing'

21

Changes in Religion: Ministers, Monarchs and Nobles

In 1558 Mary, Queen of Scots, married Francis, the heir to the French throne. In Scotland her mother, Mary of Guise, who was ruling for her as queen regent, ordered that no one was to preach the Protestant faith. John Knox preached: it was an act of rebellion. This looming figure with the long face, commanding eyes and flowing black beard thundered against the Church of Rome. People who heard him in Perth were roused by his message and began to smash the stained-glass windows and images in the town's churches. He raised his voice to stop them but he could not control them. Dundee and Ayr were two other places where Protestant ideas took hold.

Linlithgow Palace, birthplace of Mary, Queen of Scots

The regent sent for more troops from France, where her daughter Mary had become queen. Knox's main support came from the lords. They asked for help from England, now Protestant under Queen Elizabeth. She answered by sending an English fleet to the Firth of Forth and 9,000 men over the Border. Here was a change of policy indeed! English troops were in Scotland to help the Scots. The French defended the port of Leith with great skill, but in 1560 the regent died and the garrison had to surrender.

1560 was an important year. The Treaty of Edinburgh forced the French and English troops to leave Scotland. The Auld Alliance was at an end. No longer would the Scots and French fight together against the English. The Auld Alliance had led to much fighting on the Border, and sent many Scots to die on fields like Flodden. It had also kept Scotland in close touch with centres of learning in Europe. Churchmen travelled to many countries, and Scottish students went to study at the University of Paris. French words found their way into Scots – words like *fash*, *ashet* and *gardyloo*. But as Scotland became Protestant she found that she had more in common with Protestant England than with Catholic France.

A statue of John Knox preaching, situated in the courtyard of the Assembly Hall, Edinburgh, where the General Assembly meets

John Knox

John Knox became minister of St Giles in Edinburgh. Parliament met and asked the ministers to agree on what they believed. This statement, called 'The Confession of Faith', owed much to the writings of John Calvin. The ministers relied on the Bible and saw that explaining it, 'the preaching of the Word', was their main duty. The Pope's power in Scotland was to end, and Mass was not to be celebrated.

How was the new Church to be run? Knox provided his answer in *The First Book of Discipline*. He said members of each parish church were to choose their own minister. They were also to elect elders from their members every year to help to run their church. All the churches in each region were to be supervised by a senior minister called a superintendent. The affairs of the Church as a whole were to be discussed every year at a great meeting of ministers and laymen from all over Scotland. This parliament of the Church still meets, and is called the 'General Assembly'.

The nobles in Parliament agreed with these ideas, but they could not consent to the wealth of the old Church being taken over by the new one. In fact, many of the church lands were already in the hands of the very lords who were sitting in this Parliament. Because there was no money, the bold scheme John Knox had proposed – a school in every parish and a college in every town, leading on to the three universities – could not be put into practice. Scotland missed a great chance to provide schools for children all over the country.

Saints' days were no longer to be observed as holidays. To many people these had been times when they could enjoy themselves, and to them the Reformation seemed to have a solemn face.

Mary, Queen of Scots

On a misty morning in 1561 Mary, Queen of Scots, landed on Scottish soil. She had succeeded to the throne as an infant, but before she was six had been sent for safety to France, her mother's country. She was happy there, and in 1559 her husband, Francis, became King of France. Francis fell ill and died and Mary, a widow at 18, resolved to return to Scotland. She was a Catholic, and Scotland had just declared itself Protestant. On her first Sunday in Holyrood Palace she went to Mass as usual and John Knox declared that this was 'more fearful to him than if 10,000 armed enemies were landed in any part of the realm [kingdom]'.

Everything she did was criticised. Dancing and laughter in Holyrood Palace

Holyrood Palace where Mary, Queen of Scots, returned from France to live

one evening were sure to be condemned by John Knox in the pulpit of St Giles the next day. This well-educated, high-spirited, almost foreign queen was sure to need all her courage and charm to deal with scheming lords and the people in Edinburgh set against her by John Knox.

In religion she remained a faithful Catholic, but undertook to maintain the Protestant Church in Scotland. This may appear to be a strange policy for a Catholic queen, but Mary's advisers realised the power the Protestant lords and ministers had. They knew, too, that Mary Tudor had tried to make the English people Catholic again and had failed. Most important of all, Mary always hoped that she would succeed Elizabeth as queen of England or replace her one day. So she was determined never to do anything to disturb the Protestant Church.

Mary, Queen of Scots (detail from a painting attributed to François Clouet. Courtesy of the Scottish National Portrait Gallery)

Still the Protestants had reason to fear her. She removed one rival by marrying him. He was Lord Darnley, a Catholic who, after herself, was the next heir to the English throne. Plot and murder followed. Darnley was jealous of David Rizzio, the queen's Italian secretary, and was involved in the plot when Rizzio was murdered in Holyrood before the queen's eyes.

In 1567, Darnley lay ill in Kirk o' Field near Edinburgh, his body so marked with sores that he wore a mask to hide his face. There was an explosion, and 'the hous was raisett up from the ground with pouder'. Darnley was dead. It was discovered that he had been strangled before the explosion. The Earl of Bothwell, the most powerful man in Scotland, was blamed, but several others might have done it and his trial was a farce. The queen, who had been nursing Darnley, had gone back to Holyrood that evening to attend an entertainment. Had she known about the plot? We do not know, but three months later she married Bothwell.

The Protestant lords turned against them. Mary was imprisoned on an island in Loch Leven, where she was forced to give up the throne, while Bothwell left Scotland to become a pirate.

In 1568, Mary escaped with the help of a boy, young Willie Douglas, who stole the keys of the castle and rowed her to the shore. She gathered some support, but her forces were defeated at Langside near Glasgow. There was no hope for her in Scotland now. She took the risk and fled to England to throw herself on the mercy of her cousin and rival, Queen Elizabeth. She was kept in one prison or another for nearly 20 years, as English Catholics plotted to take Elizabeth's life and make Mary queen of England in her place. But it was not to be. She was tried at last for knowing about another plot, condemned to death and, as she said, 'delivered from all her cares'.

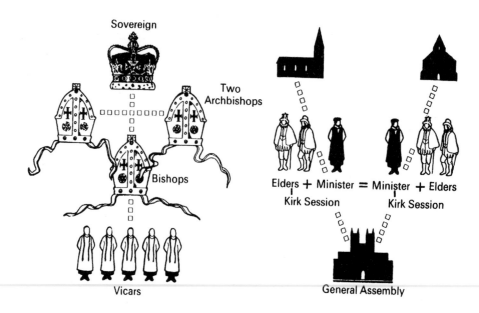

Organisation of the Church of England on the left and the Church of Scotland on the right

Andrew Melville and James VI

Many people in Scotland carried on worshipping as Catholics but the Protestant Church seemed secure. Knox was preaching with his usual fire. Even when he was so ill that he had to be helped into the pulpit, 'he was so active and vigorous that he was like to ding that pulpit in blads [break it to pieces] and fly out of it'. Mary's son, the new king James VI, was only a child, but he would be brought up as a Protestant child, educated by the great Protestant scholar, George Buchanan.

But what kind of Protestant church Scotland would have had not been settled. It could be like the Church of England, which had bishops and the queen as supreme governor. Or it could be the kind of Kirk of Scotland that Andrew Melville wanted to see.

After the death of John Knox, this fine scholar spoke for the Kirk. He believed this was not a matter for the king to settle. He told the king to his face that there were two kingdoms in Scotland – one the king's where he was master, the other Christ's 'whase subject King James the Saxt is, and of whase kingdome [is] nocht a king nor a lord, nor a heid but a member'. Merchants and craftsmen in the towns gave their support. Melville got his way in 1592, when the Presbyterian Kirk was recognised as the Church of Scotland, with complete control over its own affairs. Believing that ministers should be equal, he was against anybody being a superintendent, which reminded him of a medieval bishop. Instead, each Kirk was to have its session of elders elected for life, and each district its presbytery. Some of the ministers and elders were to meet each year in the General Assembly.

James was not yet defeated. This shambling, parentless boy had struggled to become a man. He learned to trust himself and to fear all men. He gave church lands to many of the nobles and they stopped supporting Melville. James tried to win back control of the Church by appointing bishops. But although the bishops might sit in Parliament they had no power in the Church.

John Knox had brought the Scots into the Protestant faith; he and Andrew Melville decided how the new Church would be organised. But not everyone wanted to worship in the same way, and later kings feared this Church when they had no power over it. Two struggles, one for freedom of worship and the other for control of the Church, were to be fought out in the next century.

Visits

To gain some idea of the life of kings and queens and the Scottish connection with France, explore some royal palaces, like Holyroodhouse; Stirling; Falkland in Fife; Linlithgow, west of Edinburgh. To come closer to the Protestant Reformation, go into St Giles in Edinburgh or to visit Burntisland Church in Fife.

Built after the Reformation, Burntisland Church in Fife is square with its tower in the middle, unlike Dalmeny (see page 57)

22

People in the Sixteenth Century

The Look of the Land

To modern eyes, sixteenth-century Scotland would seem a very poor country. But this was a time when towns were growing and country lairds were building themselves great towers to live in. Writers found many things to praise in parts of the country and in some towns. In the Lothians, for example, the villages were

Smailholm Tower in the Borders, built in the early sixteenth century

bigger with fertile fields around them. Clydesdale, with its coal-mines as well as good farming land, was described as 'the paradise of Scotland'. Fife, which also had good soil, had coal and salt works and busy little seaports, and was said to be like 'a grey cloth mantle [cloak] with a golden fringe'.

Edinburgh, Dundee and Aberdeen were the biggest towns, and Perth and Montrose were also busy trading places. Edinburgh, the capital, was praised for having a High Street which was as wide as a market place. Glasgow was an open town round the cathedral and a visitor wrote of it, 'This flourishing city reminds me of the beautiful fabrics [cloths or buildings] and the florid [full of flowers] fields of England.'

Country People

From about 1500 the number of people in Scotland began to increase, and kept on increasing. Most of these folk left no records, however, to tell us about their lives. Country people probably lived in the same way as their forefathers, keeping flocks and cultivating the infield, as we saw on page 65. In normal years they could produce enough to keep themselves alive.

But some years, 1594–98 for example, when grain harvests were poor, people starved. Because farmers were having to pay more for their land, food prices kept going up, even in good years. By 1600 Edinburgh families were having to pay eight times more for a loaf of bread than in 1530.

The Highlanders lived mainly on meat, milk and cheese from their herds, and fish from the rivers. In the Lowlands bread was more common. Oatmeal made porridge, brose, bannocks and oatcakes which were eaten by most of the people. Pease-meal, a flour made from ground dried peas, made up the food of the poorest.

When men were not working hard in the fields, they would be cutting wood or peat for the fire. Women were always busy grinding corn, baking on the girdle or making the family clothes.

Border Reivers

In the Borders, riding into the north of England and stealing cattle was so common that it might almost be called an industry. The men who did it were called 'Border Reivers'. Walter Scott of Harden, 'Auld Wat' as he was called, was the most famous of them. When stocks of meat were running low his wife, Mary, would lay before him at dinner-time an ashet [a serving dish] with nothing on it but a pair of spurs. This was the sign for him to lead his men over the Cheviots again. Will H. Ogilvie describes their ride in his poem, *Ho! For the Blades of Harden*:

The dark has heard them gather,
The dawn has bowed them by,
To the guard on the roof comes the drum of a hoof
And the drone of a hoof's reply.
There are more than birds on the hill to-night,
And more than winds on the plain!
The threat of the Scotts has filled the moss,
'There will be moonlight again'.

Of course, the English also crossed the Border to steal cattle, as you may read in the ballad, *Jamie Telfer of the Fair Dodhead*.

The Parson of Stobo

Before the Reformation, clergymen did not always wear dark clothes, as we learn when we meet Adam Colquhoun. He is the parson of Stobo in Peeblesshire but he lives near Glasgow Cathedral. He draws an income of two thousand pounds Scots a year (worth £400 in English money at the time) from two parishes in the upper Tweed Valley, which he visits sometimes to supervise the vicar whom he pays to take his place.

What the Parson of Stobo's hall might have been like

As he stands at the manse door to greet us, we are struck by the brightness of his clothes: the scarlet of his doublet [jacket] and waistcoat, the whiteness of his shirt, the gold trimmings on his belt and his velvet cap. Over his arm he carries a fine gown with a fur collar. He likes velvet, the most expensive of cloths, and marten, the choicest of furs.

His house is a great stone tower. It is dark as we stumble up the spiral staircase. In the hall, we admire the fine tapestries which cover the stone walls. Then we gaze at the fire, a fire of 'black stones' [coal] burning in an iron grate. In this room the parson eats at his meat-board, a table-top resting on trestles. He opens his carved cupboard to show us his treasures: 40 silver plates and vessels, two dozen silver spoons, a dozen small knives and a fork. To have all these knives and a fork is very uncommon, because men usually carry their own knives with them or use their daggers for cutting meat, and lift food with their fingers instead of using forks.

He is well off for what he calls 'belly cheer'. In his barn he has wheat, barley and oats, and in his cellar eight salted carcasses of beef, 96 salmon, six stones [about 38 kilograms] of butter, plenty of cheeses, oatmeal and herring.

He is proud of his bedroom. He sleeps in a fine, carved bed, on a soft feather mattress, with fine sheets, two plaids and two blankets to keep him warm. Curtains hang round the bed to keep out the draught. There is so much to amaze the ordinary man of Colquhoun's time: a bed which is a piece of furniture, walls whose stonework is hidden behind the tapestry hangings, the oak settle by the fireplace, the wardrobe for keeping clothes in and chests full of valuables. Suddenly there is a squawk and we shriek in terror. It's a bird, a bird of many colours with a hooked beak! The parson talks to it and tells us that it is his pet, a parrot.

Later, a change in dress took place. In 1575, ministers and their wives were ordered not to wear bright colours, embroidered clothes or jewellery. All their clothes were to be of dark colours, such as 'black, russet, sad grey, sad brown'. From this law 'clerical grey', the colour ministers are usually seen to wear, was born.

Merchants

Until 1560, Scotland and England were enemies and not much trade took place between them. Scottish merchants shipped their goods across the North Sea, especially to the Netherlands. Raw wool went to the Flemish weavers from the ports of Leith, Aberdeen and Dundee. This was by far the most valuable export and the king made money out of it, too, because after 1360 his officers collected one pound in customs duty on every sack of wool. The ports of the north-east sent out salted salmon while Pittenweem, Leith, Dumbarton, Ayr and Irvine exported herrings. Almost everything Scottish merchants sold abroad came from either farming or fishing.

One Scottish merchant, Andrew Halliburton, kept a detailed account of everything he bought and sold. Bishops, dukes and merchants were customers of his. He states in a letter in 1502 that he sold one sack of wool for 22 merks [nearly three pounds] and another sack for 23 merks, and adds, 'Hides, I think, shall be the best merchandise [things to sell] to come here at Easter for there are many folk that ask about them'. He brought back a mixture of goods in his ship: lengths of coloured cloth, books, hats, floor-tiles, wine, spices, thread for embroidery, church vessels and a tombstone.

We may say generally that Scotland gave large quantities of a few simple products in return for smaller amounts of a wide range of luxury goods.

Scottish merchants who traded abroad were ordered to be well dressed so that foreigners would think well of them. They probably were not all wealthy but they learned to look their best. Different laws were needed at home. The ordinary man in the burghs could be recognised by his 'blue bonnet and plaid' but it seems some people had been guilty of dressing too well. In 1581 families with land worth less than 2,000 merks a year (two-thirds of what Adam Colquhoun had, *see* page 116)

Huntly House in old Edinburgh, once three houses with gable ends facing the street and upstairs rooms overhanging it. Francis Spottiswood's house may have been like one of these (courtesy of Hurd Rolland Partnership, photo by Francis Caird Inglis)

were ordered not to wear cloth of gold or silver, velvet or satin or even imported wool.

Francis Spottiswood is a cloth merchant, whose shop is on the ground floor of his house in Edinburgh. He is wearing a brown coat and red stockings, but what catches our eye is his purse. It has gold tassels on it and hangs from his belt. Truly a man of money! He picks a bale of woollen cloth from the nearest chest, and unrolls it on the counter for us to inspect. When he takes us into his house, we see in the hall, or main room, a table and cupboard like the parson of Stobo's. Francis Spottiswood has also been spending his money on luxuries: a tablecloth, a silver salt-cellar and a chair for himself at the head of the table. Over in the corner is his suit of armour, his helmet and his two-handed sword. He has always to be ready to defend the town.

The bedroom is not only a place to sleep in. Mrs Spottiswood has a 'muckle wheel' in it for spinning. An important invention, the muckle wheel can spin yarn simply by turning the wheel. Mrs Spottiswood tells us how pleased she is that the old, tiring way of spinning with a spindle and whorl is dying out and that many homes now have a muckle wheel. She spins quite quickly but she has to wind the yarn by hand. 'What is that over there?' You can see yourself in it. Mrs Spottiswood calls it a 'keiking glass'.

Francis Spottiswood, the cloth merchant, also owns a horse and a plough, harrows, a cart and a sledge. Like other burgesses, he has a share in 'the burgh acres' from which most of his food comes.

By 1600 his city is bigger and busier than ever. The number of people crowded into it has risen to 8,000, not counting the children. Through its port of Leith passes most of Scotland's exports – wool, sheepskins and other skins, coal, and grain as well when harvests are good. When corn crops fail in Scotland, there is money to be made by importing grain from Baltic ports.

Schoolboys

Most boys and girls did not go to school at all. As soon as they were old enough they helped in the fields or in the house. In the burghs, boys became apprentices and learned a trade. Some boys did go to school, however, and the hours were long. At Aberdeen Grammar School, scholars had already spent two hours in class by nine o'clock in the morning. After an hour's break, they were back at their lessons until twelve o'clock, and in the afternoon they were at work from two until four and again from five o'clock until six. The main subject in grammar schools was Latin but James Melville, who went to school in Montrose, says they also studied the Bible and French, and 'be [by] our maister war teached to handle the bow for archerie, the glub for goff, the batons for fencing, also to rin, to loope, to swoom, to warsell'.

SCOTTISH TOWNS IN 1557 AND 1991 IN ORDER OF SIZE

1557 (based on taxable value)	1991 (based on census)
Edinburgh	Glasgow
Dundee	Edinburgh
Aberdeen	Aberdeen
Perth	Dundee
St Andrews	Paisley
Montrose	East Kilbride
Cupar	Dunfermline
Ayr	Greenock
Glasgow	Hamilton
Dunfermline	Cumbernauld

Visits

If you want to experience what it might have been like to live in a Border tower, visit Smailholm Tower near Kelso. Or go to Edinburgh to find out what it was like to live in a merchant's house in the sixteenth century – visit Gladstone's Land near Edinburgh Castle or Huntly House Museum down in the Canongate.

Carpenters at work (an illustration on a hoarding during the restoration of historic buildings in Stirling Castle)

23

The Struggle for Freedom during the Reign of James VI and I

STEWART RULERS OF SCOTLAND AND ENGLAND 1603–1714

James VI and I	1603–25
Charles I	1625–49
(The Commonwealth	1649–60)
Charles II	1660–85
James VII and II	1685–88
William and Mary	1689–1702 *Mary died in 1694*
Anne	1702–14

The Union of the Crowns

To the lives of most Scottish people the year 1603 brought no change. In 1603, however, Queen Elizabeth, the last of the Tudors, died. She had named James VI of Scotland to succeed her. It was a dream come true for the Scottish king. England was a powerful nation, whose sailors like Sir Francis Drake had faced the Spanish Armada and scattered or sunk its ships only 15 years before. England was a far richer country, both in crops and trade. It also had a Church after his own heart, a Church with bishops in control. 'Jamie Saxt', King of Scotland, became James I, King of England without a blow struck in anger. Little wonder he felt that God was on his side!

James and his courtiers departed for London, the capital of his greater kingdom. He was not sorry to leave Scotland. For years the nobles had struggled to control him, and the ministers of the Kirk had declared from their pulpits that he had no control over them. He was to come back to Scotland only once in the next 22 years. Only the merchants of Edinburgh were sorry to see him go, as many of his nobles went with him and would buy their wines, cloth and other luxuries in London in future.

Although all of Great Britain was now under one king, Scotland and England remained separate in other ways. They kept their own systems of law. Their Churches were different; the Church of England was Episcopalian, that is, governed by bishops, but in Scotland the Kirk was Presbyterian, with kirk sessions and General Assembly. The bishops James had appointed in Scotland sat in Parliament, but at first they had no power in the Kirk. Each country kept its own parliament. James tried to bring the two nations closer together, but the English Parliament did not agree to his proposals.

James and England

James had trouble with the English Parliament from the start. Parliament said that the king could not make laws or tax people if it did not agree. If the king did not recognise its rights it could cut off his supply of money. Parliament was now demanding far more from a foreign king like James than it had dared from Queen Elizabeth.

In James's time, no one thought that all men should be free to worship as they pleased. They could not have imagined that we would have many different churches today, or that people would be able to go to any church they liked. This is called religious toleration, but in the seventeenth century, each group believed it was the only one which worshipped in the right way, and each tried to convert all the others to its beliefs and services.

Many English people were Puritans. They lived strict lives, they liked to read the Bible and wanted to worship in a simple manner. When James met some of

Edinburgh Castle where James VI was born

James VI of Scotland, and I of England after 1603 (detail from a painting by an unknown artist. Courtesy of the Scottish National Portrait Gallery)

them at Hampton Court in 1604, they had high hopes of him. Coming from Scotland he would surely make some of the changes that they wanted to see in the Church of England. But when they mentioned Presbytery, where, as he said, 'Tom and Will and Dick may meet and censure [find fault with] me', James was furious. They reminded him of the struggles he had had with the Kirk in Scotland. He refused to let them have their own way, but he did agree to a new translation of the Bible being made. This, the *Authorised Version* as it is known, is still used by Protestants today. It is addressed to him, calling him 'the Most High and Mighty Prince, James, by the Grace of God, King of Great Britain, France and Ireland, Defender of the Faith'.

In 1620, some Puritans known as the 'Pilgrim Fathers' set sail from Plymouth in the ship *Mayflower*. They braved the wild Atlantic to seek their freedom in America.

Roman Catholics in England, knowing that his mother had been a Catholic, were also disappointed in James. The plot by some Catholics to blow up the king and Parliament with gunpowder was discovered, and Guy Fawkes was arrested in a cellar on 4 November 1605. Nowadays, before the Queen opens Parliament, the Yeomen of the Guard always inspect the cellars. The Fifth of November, when the Houses of Parliament were to have been blown up, is still celebrated as 'Guy Fawkes Night'.

James and Scotland

Even from London, James was able to rule Scotland easily, through men who would do what he told them. He was sure that the Scottish Parliament would obey him, because 'his men' were members of a group called the 'Committee of the Articles'. It decided which 'articles' or bills pleased the king, and passed them on to Parliament which met simply to agree to them. James spoke the truth when he declared:

> This I must say for Scotland and may truly vaunt [boast] it. Here I sit and govern it with my pen. I write and it is done, and by a Clerk of the Council I govern Scotland now, which others could not do by the sword.

He worked away quietly to try to gain control over the Church of Scotland. The General Assembly had been the place where the ministers and elders made their voices heard, but he would not let it meet. He appointed bishops and gave them the real power. These things made him feel he was master over the Kirk. His next step was to bring in the same kind of church service as was used in the Church of England. People were told, for example, to kneel down when they were taking Communion. But it was one thing to make changes: it was far more difficult to make people obey them, as Charles I, James's son, was soon to discover.

Visits

If you are in Aberdeenshire you can explore another aspect of James VI's reign – castles with a style of their own. Choose from Castle Fraser, Craigievar and Crathes (all west of Aberdeen). They are all in the care of the National Trust for Scotland.

24

The Struggle for Freedom: Charles I and Cromwell

When Charles I became king in 1625, he was the first king of Scotland to be more an Englishman than a Scot. He ruled from London as his father had done, but he did not know the Scots and did not understand the Church of Scotland. The Scottish Parliament did what he wanted: it was the Kirk he had most to fear.

Soon he made other enemies. Many of the Scottish nobles had lands which had once belonged to the Church. Their families had held them so long that they thought they owned them. But by an act in 1625 it looked as if the new king was trying to take them all back for himself. This was not true, but the damage was done and many of the nobles turned against the king.

Riot when the new prayer book was read in St Giles, 1637
(by courtesy of Edinburgh City Libraries)

Charles and the Church in Scotland

Charles ordered that a new Scottish prayer book, like the one used in the Church of England, be read in all the churches in Scotland. He did not think of asking a General Assembly what they thought of it. Its first reading in St Giles in Edinburgh was met by a shower of stools and stones when riots broke out. This was the first sign that the ordinary people would stand up against the king.

In 1638, the National Covenant was drawn up and signed in Greyfriars' Kirk in Edinburgh. Then, all over the southern half of the country, people eagerly put their names to copies. Those who signed were the Covenanters. They promised to defend 'the true religion', that is, the practices of the Church of Scotland, and also to defend the king. You may think that it would be impossible for them to carry out both these promises, since the king seemed to be attacking the Church of Scotland. Most people, however, believed that it was William Laud, the Archbishop of Canterbury, who was giving advice and who brought in the new Prayer Book. The time would come when those who signed the Covenant had to decide which was their greater loyalty – to their king or to their Church. Most of them chose to fight for the Kirk; some, led by the Marquis of Montrose, preferred to do their duty to the king.

This is how the Scots challenged the king. They were about to fight a war for their religion, like the Thirty Years' War (1618–48) which was going on in Europe. Many of their leaders were battle-hardened soldiers who had fought in that war. They had been 'soldiers of fortune' in the armies of Gustavus Adolphus, the Protestant king of Sweden. Their leader was the 'old, little, crooked soldier', Alexander Leslie, who had risen to command the Swedish forces in Germany after Gustavus was killed. The Covenanters soon had a strong army of 20,000 men. Most of them were 'stout young plewmen . . . Had ye lent your eare in the morning, or especialle at even, and heard in the tents the sound of some singing psalms, some praying and some reading scripture, you would have been refreshed.'

When they advanced into England Charles did not have an army strong enough to stop them. He had to make peace and allow them to have their own Kirk again. He had lost control of Scotland completely.

The Covenanters and the Civil War

Early in his reign, Charles had quarrelled with the English Parliament, and for the next 11 years (1629–40) he had been ruling without it. Now, because he needed extra money to pay for an army, he had to call Parliament again. Parliament wanted to reduce the power he had and stop him ruling on his own again. The two sides could not agree, and the Civil War in England broke out.

Charles's followers, the Cavaliers, came from the ranks of the country landowners and their men, while Parliament's army, nicknamed 'Roundheads', consisted mainly of craftsmen and merchants from the towns, and prosperous farmers like Oliver Cromwell. Most of the Roundheads were Puritans, and some were Presbyterians like the Scots.

The two sides were evenly matched: the support of the Scottish army could tip the scales. The Covenanters agreed to fight on Parliament's side, if the religion of England was changed 'according to the word of God and the example of the best reformed Churches'. To the Scots, that meant the Presbyterian Church. They had started fighting against the king because he tried to force his religion on them: the Scots were now trying to force a Church like their own on the English people. In 1644, at Marston Moor in Yorkshire, the Scottish foot-soldiers helped Oliver Cromwell's magnificent cavalry, the Ironsides, to victory over the Cavaliers.

Meanwhile, the Marquis of Montrose, who had signed the National Covenant, decided he could not set aside his oath to defend the king. He raised a small army of Irishmen and Highlanders to fight for King Charles in Scotland, and swept through the land like a whirlwind. Thanks to the speed with which he moved his men, their toughness and his own gifts as a leader, he won six victories in a single year between September 1644 and August 1645. Scotland was in his hand. He was ready to invade England to help the king. But the Covenanters under David Leslie surprised his little army at Philiphaugh near Selkirk and practically wiped them out.

Successes at Philiphaugh in Scotland and at Naseby in England made 1645 a year of victory for Cromwell's army and the Covenanters. Four years later Charles I, a prisoner of the Parliamentary army, was tried by Parliament and put to

Doon Hill on the right, the strong position above Dunbar the Covenanters gave up in 1650 to be slaughtered on the low ground by Cromwell's army

death on the scaffold. Horror spread among the Scottish people. Many of them had wanted their own religion, but not at the expense of the life of the king. At once they proclaimed his son, Charles II, king of Scotland, but England became a republic, known as the Commonwealth, without a king.

Cromwell and Scotland

In 1650 Cromwell's army marched north into Scotland. At Dunbar, the Covenanters and the Roundheads, who had been comrades-in-arms at Marston Moor, came face to face in battle. The Covenanters were placed in such a strong position on Doon Hill by David Leslie that Cromwell did not dare attack them. Then the ministers who were with the army persuaded him to move his men down the hill. This was just what Cromwell wanted. 'The Lord has delivered them into our hands,' he said, as he sent his Ironsides crashing through the Scottish lines. Another Scottish army invaded England and, exactly a year later, on 3 September 1651, Cromwell crushed it at the battle of Worcester.

English troops under General Monk kept Scotland quiet. Even in the Highlands, order was kept as it never had been before. As an Englishman observed, 'A man may ride all over Scotland with a switch in his hand and a hundred pounds in his pocket, which he could not have done these five hundred years.' Everyone was given freedom of worship, not that the Church of Scotland wanted this. Scotland also had the right to send members to the new British Parliament in London, but the Scots knew that Scotland and England were held together only by the force of Cromwell's armies.

Cromwell's house at Ely, Cambridgeshire

25

The Struggle for Freedom: Restoration to Revolution

When Cromwell died in 1658, there was no strong man to succeed him. General Monk, the commander of the Commonwealth forces in Scotland, was convinced that only the king's return would satisfy the people. He marched his men to London, and recalled Charles II from exile. This ended Britain's only experiment of ruling without a king.

The Restoration, as the return of the king was called, took place in 1660. It was an occasion for much rejoicing. The king was back, and Scotland was a separate country once more. But soon the people ceased to rejoice.

Charles II and the Church

Charles controlled Scotland, as his grandfather had done, 'with the pen'. He appointed bishops to rule the Church and declared the National Covenant illegal. He gave local landowners the right to choose ministers. As a result, 262 ministers who had not been appointed in this way, mainly in the south-west of Scotland, left their churches. There, and round about Edinburgh, people gathered outside to join them in worship in conventicles among the hills.

John Blackadder was a minister who once preached to an assembly of 4,000 people near Cramond; John Welsh was the great-grandson of John Knox; for 20 years Alexander Peden lived and preached in the open air, and Richard Cameron held out to the last. Troops were sent to arrest these 'outed' ministers but many people, risking fines and horrible torture, came to hear them. Ministers and people suffered, but they took courage from the word of God: 'Blessed are they which are persecuted for righteousness' sake: for theirs is the kingdom of heaven.'

A Conventicle

Imagine the folk setting off from the distant village, some walking, some riding, the men carrying weapons, until they reach the appointed hollow in the hills. Sentries are posted to look out in all directions for the hated red-coats. The

Sandy Peden's mask (courtesy of the Trustees of the National Museums of Scotland)

women pull heather to sit on. 'There now, see that man in black, pulling off his mask. That's the minister, that's Sandy Peden.'

He leads them in worship, talking to them in homely, simple terms. 'I will tell you where the Church is,' he says. 'It is wherever a praying young man or young women is; at a dykeside in Scotland. That is where the Church is.'

The service is not interrupted today by the shout of the sentry or the warning cry of the peewit, and when it is over the people return quietly to their homes. The wandering Peden goes to share a meal with them, but will not let them risk being caught giving him shelter at night. Instead he sleeps under the stars.

The Covenanters Fight

People rose up against these laws. They marched in the rain from Galloway and Ayrshire towards Edinburgh, a brave little army, but armed mainly with scythes and pitchforks. In 1666, at Rullion Green in the Pentland Hills, royalist forces under Dalyell of the Binns overwhelmed them. Prisoners were tortured and some hanged. This was a 'reign of terror', as soldiers under Dalyell and Graham of Claverhouse scoured the country in search of Covenanters. For a time after this it was made easier for the covenanting ministers to come back into the Church and nearly a hundred did.

Then in 1679, a handful of Covenanters dragged Archbishop Sharp from his coach on Magus Muir near St Andrews and killed him before his daughter's eyes. Sharp had been a Presbyterian minister, but had deserted to the king's side to become a bishop. Both sides gathered troops and a large government army won the battle at Bothwell Bridge. A thousand Covenanters were taken prisoner and marched to Edinburgh. Most were pardoned on condition that they would not rebel again, but over 200 of them were transported to the colonies.

A few extreme rebels held out. They were called 'Cameronians' after their leader, Richard Cameron, and were hunted down and put to death. Others were cruelly dealt with. In 1685, for example, Margaret Wilson, a girl of 18, and Margaret MacLachlan were tied to stakes on the Solway and were believed to have been drowned. People like these, who died for what they believed, were martyrs and are remembered in the famous lines by Robert Louis Stevenson:

Blows the wind to-day, and the sun and the rain are flying,
Blows the wind on the moors to-day and now,
Where about the graves of the martyrs the whaups [curlews] are crying
My heart remembers how!

Grey recumbent [flat] tombs of the dead in desert places,
Standing stones on the vacant wine-red moor,
Hills of sheep, and the homes of the silent vanished races,
And winds austere and pure.

Be it granted me to behold you again in dying,
Hills of home! And to hear again the call;
Hear about the graves of the martyrs the peewees [lapwings] crying,
And hear no more at all.

'The Glorious Revolution'

The next king, James VII and II, was a Roman Catholic. In 1687 he issued the first of two Declarations of Indulgence, which let Presbyterians and Roman Catholics, as well as members of the Church of England, worship freely. It seemed a sensible way to end so much torture and killing, but perhaps James's main aim was just to help the Roman Catholics. In England, he put Roman Catholics in high positions in the State and in the Army, although this was against the law. When his son was born in 1688, people feared that rule by Catholic kings would go on and on in what was mainly a Protestant country. William of Orange, James's son-in-law, was asked to come over from Holland to save Protestantism in Britain.

William came, and James fled. William, and his wife Mary, became king and queen of England by agreeing to the Bill of Rights in 1689. Since that time the ruler has had to be Protestant, and has not been able to rule as he likes. For raising taxes, having an army in peace time, altering old laws or passing new ones, the king or queen has had to work through Parliament. He or she has no power to do any of these things without asking Parliament. As a result, Parliament has become the partner the sovereign cannot do without in governing the country. This great change, which took place peacefully in England, was known as 'The Glorious, Bloodless Revolution'.

In Scotland also, William and Mary became joint rulers. The Committee of the Articles, which earlier kings had used to keep the Scottish Parliament in check, was abolished in 1690, and Scotland gained a Parliament which, for the first time, was free to propose and debate new laws. In the Highlands, however, Graham of Claverhouse (now Viscount Dundee) raised the clans for James. He defeated the government troops at the battle of Killiecrankie (1689), but when he himself was killed the rebellion came to an end.

Scotland gained the Presbyterian Church most people wanted. The bishops were deposed and the Church was free of royal control. The General Assembly met in 1690, for the first time since the days of Cromwell, and has met every year since. The Kirk had won its struggle against the king. Religious toleration was granted to members of other Protestant Churches, and people began to think that it was right that everyone should be free to worship as he or she pleased.

Visits

If you would like to find out more about the Covenanters go to Greenhill, near Biggar in Lanarkshire – it is one of the many display centres run by Biggar Museum Trust and is well worth a visit. While you are there, why not investigate the church section in the town's Moat Park heritage centre. Wider in scope is the St Mungo Museum of Religious Life and Art in Castle Street, Glasgow, near the Cathedral (*see* the map on page 198).

Canongate Kirk (1688–89), built for the congregation driven out of the Abbey Church of Holyrood by James VII

26

Life in the Highlands in the Seventeenth Century

In the last 200 years, great numbers of people have left the Highlands. Nowadays every summer sees people from southern Scotland, England, the USA and Commonwealth countries like Canada, Australia and New Zealand returning to visit the glens of their ancestors.

Let us take a look at the old way of life of the Highlanders, as it was in the seventeenth century.

The Highland Line separated Highlanders who spoke Gaelic from Lowlanders who did not. It runs along the edge of the Highlands where they drop down to the Lowlands, roughly 30 kilometres north of Glasgow, Stirling, Perth and Montrose. It continues northwards and westwards, leaving out most of Aberdeenshire and the flatter lands along the Moray Firth. The Highlanders live north and west of the Highland Line.

Chiefs and Clans

The Highlanders belonged to clans, each under its own chief. The word 'clan', which means 'the children', suggests that the members of one clan were all related to one another. Certainly, the chief was like an all-powerful father over them. They paid him rents and labour services. He was their judge and his word was law. He was their commander, who could call the clan to war by sending round the 'fiery cross', charred in fire and smeared with blood. His relatives held their land directly from him. They all had the clan surname, but other men might be in the clan because they were on land the clan had taken. Macintyres, for example, were members of the Clan Campbell.

The chief held the clan land. He kept some, called 'mensal land', for himself, he gave pieces to personal attendants like the bard, the harper and the piper, and split the rest on 'tack', or lease, to his relatives, the tacksmen. They paid low rents and let their land to sub-tenants, who paid for it by working the tacksmen's land and looking after their cattle. This made the tacksmen sure of getting a living without having to work. They were the most important members of the clan and the chief fighting men.

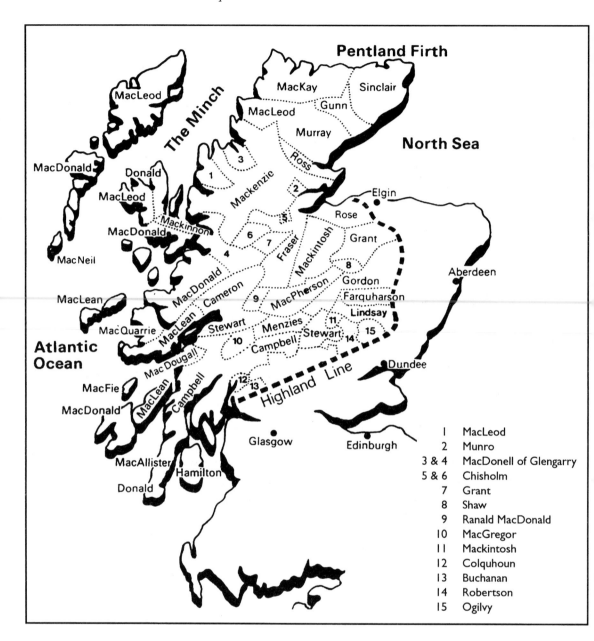

1	MacLeod
2	Munro
3 & 4	MacDonell of Glengarry
5 & 6	Chisholm
7	Grant
8	Shaw
9	Ranald MacDonald
10	MacGregor
11	Mackintosh
12	Colquhoun
13	Buchanan
14	Robertson
15	Ogilvy

Clan map of Scotland

Bards and others kept clan memories alive by telling stories about heroes of old or recent times, or by composing poems or singing songs to entertain at a *ceilidh*, or gathering. Seldom were these written down: people simply learned them by listening. The MacCrimmon family in Skye also developed the classical bagpipe music, called *pibroch*, and taught it to pipers from other clans.

Making a Living

The poorer clansmen were far worse off. It is recorded that in the Western Isles before 1600 'no labourers of the ground are permitted to steir furth of the cuntrie [leave where they lived] quhatevir their masters have ado, except only gentlemen quhilk labouris not, that the labour belonging to the teiling of the ground and the wynning of thair corns may not be left undone'.

The main job for the men was looking after their animals. They had to herd their cattle and sheep constantly to protect them from raiders and wild animals like foxes and wolves[1]. Highland cattle, called 'black cattle' but sometimes reddish or dark-brown in colour, were the Highlanders' main source of wealth. In May the herds drove them to the hill pastures for the summer. The women and girls went to live in the shielings up there, and made butter and cheese. In September drovers took many of the beasts to be sold at the Cattle Tryst at Crieff, because there was not enough feeding to keep them all through the winter. Highland cows did not give much milk, only a Scots pint (about two litres) a day, compared with over 18 litres from a good Ayrshire cow today. Sheep, too, were milked, besides providing a little fine wool which was used to clothe the Highlanders.

Not much of the land was good for growing crops. Some pieces of land were cultivated with a wooden plough pulled by four highland ponies, and in patches higher up with a caschrom (*see* page 158). From oats they made oatcakes and porridge, and from barley they were able to produce whisky, but the Highlanders, who never grew enough corn for themselves, bartered butter or cattle for grain with the Lowland farmers.

Clans nearest to the Lowlands often stole cattle and drove them home. Sometimes they levied blackmail (took money) in return for a promise to protect a farmer's cattle. A letter written by Cameron of Lochiel shows how common cattle raids were. His men had been accused of raiding a farm belonging to one of the Grants, but Lochiel protested, 'My men were not in your bounds, but in Murray [Moray] lands where all men take their prey.'

Weapons and Dress

Feuds between one clan and another, cattle-reiving and droving, all required the Highlander to be a fighter. His chief weapon was a basket-hilted broadsword. It left him one hand free, and he carried on his left arm a targe (shield) and in his left hand a dirk (dagger). His round targe, covered with studded leather, had a long spike in the centre. He could use it to attack as well as defend himself. Armed like this, Highlanders in war liked to be on high ground and charge down on their enemies.

[1] The last wolf was killed in 1743

Highlanders wearing belted plaids in different ways (courtesy of the Trustees of the National Library of Scotland)

A man's main garment was the plaid or 'great wrap'. He wrapped it round his waist and threw the remainder over his shoulder. He could also wear it to cover the upper part of his body like a cloak. The plaid acted as a blanket as well. It could be difficult to fight in, and before an attack the Highlanders took off their plaids and charged in their shirts. Women wore home-dyed dresses of wool and linen, with a checked plaid over their shoulders. At this time no clan turned out all wearing the same tartan. In battle all the men from the same clan simply wore the same emblem in their bonnets. The MacDonalds of Clanranald, for example, wore heather and the Frasers sprigs of yew.

Homes

The Highland house had thick walls of stones built without cement and a thatched roof. Since he spent most of his life out of doors, the Highlander thought of his house as a shelter from the rain and the cold, a shelter for both man and beast. His cow was valuable to him and occupied the byre at one end of the house. The door, often the only outside door, opened into the byre, and to reach the living quarters he passed through a lobby between two box-beds into the kitchen. There a peat-fire burned, warming the cooking-pot which hung by a chain from the rafters. If there was another 'little room' it would be separated from the kitchen only by a wooden partition.

Box-beds with heather to lie on, a few three-legged stools and a bench to sit on, were usually the only articles of furniture. The women spun with spindles and whorls by the glint of the fire. The family sat 'round the fire' on stools or flat stones, with one for any wanderer who might want to come in.

The people lived in small settlements: there were few towns. Until 1641 most Highland trade was in the hands of the Inverness merchants. Gradually, markets and fairs were started in new burghs like Wick and Dingwall or places like Portree, where two fairs were held each year after 1693. Highland women might want ribbons, spoons, wooden plates, combs and shears, but they had little to sell in return: a cheese or two, a little butter or some woollen cloth. For most of them, the wandering chapman or pedlar supplied all they could afford from the outside world.

King, Churches and Clans

It was always difficult to make the Highlanders obey the king's laws. When the MacGregors killed a great many of the clan Colquhoun in 1603, James VI decided to root out the whole of that clan. He hanged a dozen of them and put a price on the heads of others. They had all to take new surnames in order to stay alive.

The Bishop of Iona got the chiefs in the west to agree to the Statutes of Iona in 1609. They promised to stop fighting other clans and to make their men faithful

The fireplace at Voe Croft Museum, Shetland. The fire is burning peat
and the pieces of furniture are all made from driftwood

members of his kind of Protestant Church, a church with bishops. The Roman Catholic Church kept its hold over other clans, like the MacDonalds, with the help of preachers who came across from Ireland. As a result, many of the Highlanders, with the notable exception of the Campbells, belonged to different churches from the one the Convenanters were fighting for in the south.

Visits

Two places which are easy to reach via the A9 north to Inverness are recommended: Blair Castle at Blair Atholl was the home of a great Highland chief, and the Highland Folk Museum at Kingussie has a marvellous collection of everyday things which illustrate the daily life of Highland people in the seventeenth century.

Walkers resting in the ruins of a shieling hut in Lewis, formerly the summer home of women who tended the cattle on higher pastures

27

Life in the Burghs in the Seventeenth Century

During the seventeenth century, over a hundred new burghs of barony were founded. Many of them had been the main village on a lord's land and were given the right to hold a market. If they were good centres, they might sometimes win trade from a nearby royal burgh. From 1672, the new burghs were also given the right to trade abroad if they wished.

There were many burghs in Fife. As Sir Walter Scott's character, Andrew Fairservice, said, 'There's the Kingdom of Fife, frae Culross to the East Neuk, it's just like a great combined city, sae mony royal burghs yoked end on end.' These ports faced the Forth and traded across the North Sea.

Culross (pronounced 'Cooris') grew up beside an abbey. It became a royal burgh in 1588, and was a flourishing little port exporting coal and salt. The Civil War, and the wars with the Dutch and then the French, interrupted Scotland's trade so much that at the end of the century Fletcher of Saltoun was driven to declare that 'the Fife seaports once very prosperous are in our day little better than so many heaps of ruins.'

Plan of seventeenth century Culross (the Town House tower is later)

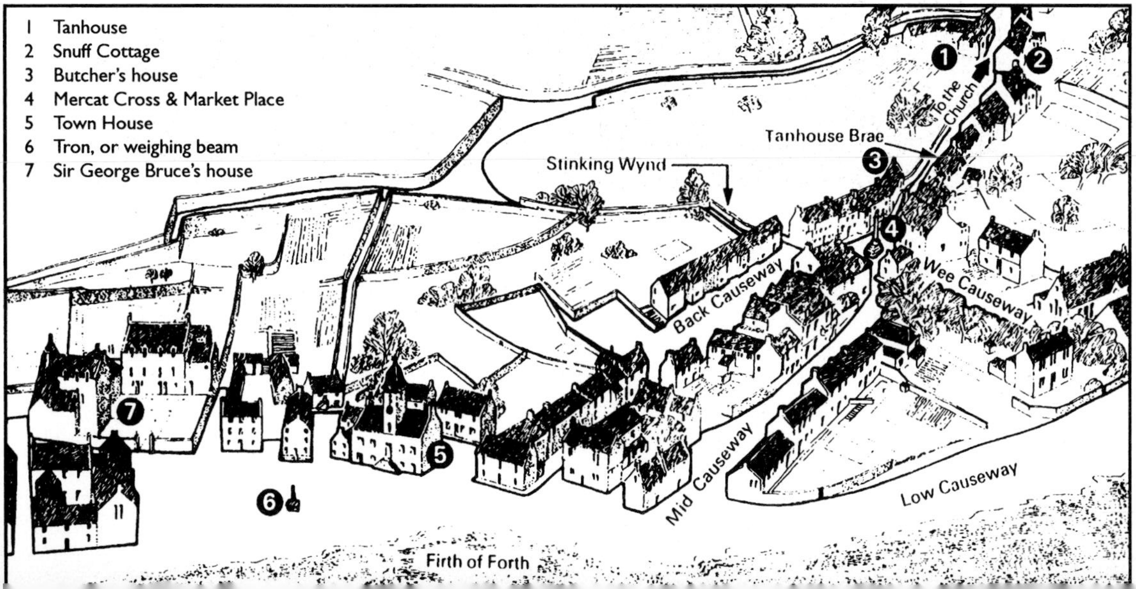

1 Tanhouse
2 Snuff Cottage
3 Butcher's house
4 Mercat Cross & Market Place
5 Town House
6 Tron, or weighing beam
7 Sir George Bruce's house

When its coal ran out after 1700, the other industries declined and Culross fell asleep. During the twentieth century, the National Trust for Scotland restored many of its old buildings, and have kept alive this seventeenth-century burgh for us to see today.

The Busy Burgh of Culross

Visiting it now, you step back in time – you are in a seventeenth-century burgh. Walk up the narrow streets and you will see that they are highest in the centre where there is a row of flat stones to walk on. Cobble stones from the beach have been laid on each side, sloping down to the gutters. The middle of the road, the 'croon of the causeway' as it is called, is the best place to walk, out of the water and rubbish. The merchants walk on the 'croon' and expect apprentices and other people to stand aside to let them pass.

The houses are close together, shielding each other from the wind. They are built of stone with low doorways and little windows. The walls of some are painted in pleasant colours and many of the gable ends have crow-steps, a zig-zag of stones leading up to the chimney. The masons built like this to keep the house dry where the roof meets the gable-end. Lums, or chimneys, are set in the end of the house. The roofs are made of bright orange tiles from Holland but some houses are still covered with thatch.

In Sir George Bruce's house note the crowsteps, the top windows with glass above and wooden shutters below, and the forestairs, lower left

Sir George Bruce is the driving force in the burgh. He has bought up 40 of the salt-pans, which use up a great deal of coal.

Along the shore, sea-water is trapped in ponds at high tide. Some of the water evaporates in the heat of the sun. Poured into rows of flat iron pans, the salty water is heated over coal fires. Steam belches forth until all the water has boiled away. Men shovel the salt into baskets and cart them off to storehouses ready for export. Bruce's workers are now producing over 90 tonnes of salt a week.

Bruce also has a coal-mine which is one of the marvels of Scotland. It has two shafts, and miners can go up or down either on land, or out in the sea. A round stone tower has been built out in the Forth, higher than the level of high tide. Down these two shafts, the miners cut through the rock into a rich seam of coal. They have made a huge tunnel, curved in the shape of an arch and high enough for a man to stand up in. Many side-cuttings branch out from it, like side-streets and closes in a town. There men cut coal, in faint candlelight, out under the sea. Water seeping through the roof makes the mine wet. Three horses move round and round working a chain of 36 buckets which bring the water up to the surface and pour it back into the sea. (This mine was flooded and wrecked in a great storm in 1625.)

Coal and salt, land and trade make Sir George Bruce rich. The miners and salters are his serfs. They have not become free like most townsmen and peasants. Wives and sons follow the men down the mine. No member of the family can escape to another trade. (Miners did not become free until 1799.)

Where the smiths are working, the clang of their hammers is deafening! They take a lump of hot iron and keep hammering it until they have made it flat and round. When they have joined on a handle at the side, they have made 'a guid Culross griddle' or girdle. James VI came and watched them at work in 1599 and he gave them the sole right of making girdles like these in Scotland. The mark they put on each one, the crown and the hammer, shows where it came from. Housewives at home and abroad like them for baking oatcakes and oatmeal bannocks on the fire.

Other craftsmen, too, are busy. The tanners are working on skins and leather at the top of Tanhouse Brae; the shoemakers and weavers have work to finish for next week's market at the Mercat Cross. Often we can tell by the smell where some men work, the butchers and bakers for example, but sometimes they mark their houses with the signs of their trade. A carving of a cleaver and a spring balance on a stone in the wall tell us where the Culross butcher lives. Up the hill lives the snuff-maker, who grinds tobacco into a fine powder. Many people like to sniff it up their noses. Some words above his door show his surprise at the new craze, and they might hint at more:

Wha' would ha' thocht it
Noses would ha' bocht it.

A man is being hustled up the steps of the Town House. A red-faced man is complaining, 'I sold him a fine pair of breeks last week and he hasn't paid me a penny.'

'Save your breath for the Council,' commands the bailie who made the arrest. The case is heard by the Council and the man, found guilty, is locked in the debtor's room. If he had been guilty of any other crime he would have been put in the prison below the council chamber. When he does not come out along with the Council, the people know that this is another case of a man who had not paid his debts.

Not far from the Town House is Sir George Bruce's home, the finest in Culross. He just calls it 'The Collier's House' but it shows that he had money to spend. It is a big house, which has doubled in size during his lifetime. An old mason is busy chiselling 'S. G. B.', the initials for Sir George Bruce, on a stone for the top of a dormer window. Glaziers are preparing lattice windows, fitting the diamond-shaped glass together with strips of lead. The windows are not made to open and shut, but below the glass part of each window are two little doors or shutters which open to let in the air. All the bedrooms are lined with the finest Baltic pine and painted with bright patterns and pictures. We hear that Sir George Bruce plans to employ an artist to paint more Biblical scenes on the ceilings.

Down in the harbour, men are loading cartloads of coals on board ships bound for ports in Holland, Germany and the Baltic. A carter has just brought linen yarn and bales of cloth from Dunfermline, and will carry back timber just unloaded from Norway.

Traders and Manufacturers

On the whole, the main cargoes Scottish traders sent abroad were skins and hides, as well as wool, linen and woollen cloth, salt herrings and salmon. Gradually coal was becoming the most popular export to the Netherlands and many Dutch ships came over to collect it. In the past, the Scots had sent most of their goods to the Netherlands, especially to the port of Campvere where they were given more freedom to trade than they had with England. Many Scottish families settled in Campvere. There was also a Scottish lodging-house where Scottish merchants on a visit would stay, and they could worship in their own church. It was Thomas Cunningham, a merchant in Campvere, who sent to Scotland the weapons the Covenanters needed in the Civil War. As Scottish merchants began to send more ships to trade with ports on the Baltic, such as Stockholm and Danzig, others went out to live there or in towns in Poland.

Merchants in different Scottish burghs had their ups and downs in trade. The fishing ports of Fife sold fewer fish in Holland, while other ports like Culross sent out more coal and salt. In the west, Glasgow men started new industries and were building up their trade, especially to Ireland, and risking a smuggling trip now and then to America. Edinburgh was still by far the richest town: its port of Leith handled most of Scotland's basic exports and one-third of all imports, including most of the wine.

In the 1680s Parliament did its best to help new Scottish firms make things in Scotland, such as sugar, soap, gunpowder and pottery, as well as cloth. So that the Scottish cloth-makers could have the home market to themselves, it passed an act to stop all kinds of cloth coming in from abroad. Near Haddington, the New Mills Company started to make fine cloth on a large scale. The place was a hive of industry for several years, but it could not make enough cloth for the whole of Scotland. After the Union of 1707 English merchants could again send good quality cloth north free of duty. The New Mills could not sell theirs so cheaply and before long they had to close down.

Visits

Culross lies to the east of the Kincardine Bridge and west of the Forth Road Bridge, and can be reached by bus from Dunfermline.

Other old seaports worth exploring are situated east of Kirkcaldy and Elie – St Monans (visit the restored windmill with its excellent explanation of salt-making), Anstruther (with its famous fisheries museum), Pittenweem (fishing) and Crail, all with harbours formerly trading across the North Sea.

Tools on the gravestones in Culross churchyard give clues to the occupations of a girdle smith (TOP) and a butcher (BOTTOM)

28

The Union of Scotland and England

In 1690, the Scottish Parliament became free and could begin to do things for the benefit of the Scottish people, even if they were not in the best interests of England.

The Scots had one constant grudge against the English. Compared with England, Scotland was poor with no colonies and little trade. In spite of the Union of the Crowns, she was considered by England to be a foreign country and could not trade with England or the English colonies without paying duties. At this time countries tried to produce all the goods they needed for themselves, and kept out foreign goods by putting on heavy duties. If they had colonies abroad, they kept all the trade with them for themselves.

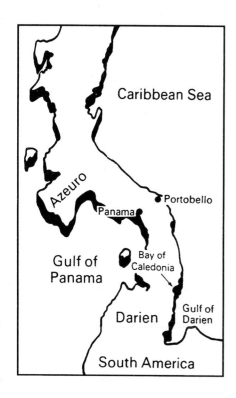

Darien

The Darien Scheme

Scotland's foreign trade was drying up and some merchants decided to start a colony of their own. In 1695 they formed a company, 'The Company of Scotland Trading to Africa and the Indies', and were given the right to trade between Scotland and America, Africa and Asia for 31 years. William Paterson had a plan, and they thought he ought to know all about making money, as he had just helped to found the Bank of England. A great many landowners and merchants invested their savings – £150,000 in all – in the new venture. Darien, on the narrow strip of land joining North and South America, was the place Paterson chose for this great centre of buying and selling by the Scots.

Paterson had not considered all the problems of setting up a colony there: the heat, malaria, the need to break in the land for crops, or the Spaniards who claimed that the land was theirs. Not enough thought was given to what people would want to buy there, and there was little demand for the heavy cloths, stockings and wigs they took out. The Spaniards who had settled in Central America did not want to share their trade with any other country. When the Scots turned to the English in Jamaica for help, they were astounded when none was given. But why should the English help Scotsmen to start a colony which would be competing with their own traders? This Scottish scheme also interfered with William III's plans to keep Spain friendly.

The Darien Scheme was a dismal failure. Hundreds of settlers lost their lives and all the money was gone. In their misery the Scots put the blame not on their mistakes, but on the king and the English merchants. The Union of the Crowns was never nearer to breaking point.

The Massacre of Glencoe

The Highlanders already had reason to hate the king. Their chiefs had been made to swear an oath of loyalty to William and Mary. The deadline was 31 December 1691. To some of the chiefs, it was a matter of honour to be slow in taking the oath. MacIan, chief of the MacDonalds of Glencoe, reported in time to the commander of the troops at Fort William, who told him that he should have gone to Inveraray to take the oath before the sheriff. MacIan was old, the weather was miserable, and he struggled through the snow to Inveraray. He had to wait until the sheriff arrived, and he took the oath on 6 January 1692. The sheriff seemed satisfied, and the old chief thought his duty done.

Sir John Dalrymple, the Master of Stair, who had the most power in Scotland at the time, was delighted when he heard that MacIan had been late. Here was a chance to make an example of a small clan. A hundred and twenty soldiers, led by Campbell of Glenlyon, a deadly enemy of the MacDonalds, arrived in the glen. They came in peace, they said, and were kindly treated at the tables and firesides of the MacDonalds for nearly a fortnight. After ten days there, Campbell of Glenlyon received this order:

> You are hereby ordered to fall upon the rebels, the MacDonalds of Glencoe, and put all to the sword under seventy. You are to have a special care that the old fox and his sons do upon no account escape your hands.

Before light one February morning, they struck. The chief was shot in his bed, and 38 men, as well as women and children were put to the sword, while others struggled through the snow to safety among the Stewarts of Appin.

Many questions about the massacre were left unanswered. Who was to blame? Was it Dalrymple, the Master of Stair? Was he the planner or the faithful royal servant? Was it the king? He signed the order, but did he understand what was to happen? One thing is certain: this action turned the Highlanders against 'Dutch William' and his government.

'The Ill Years'

From 1695 onwards the crops failed, and the people called that time 'the seven ill years'. Harvests were so late that harvesting was still going on in January. Food was dear, and many people died from cold and hunger. An eye-witness tells us, 'I have seen when meal was all sold in markets, women clapping their hands and tearing the clothes off their heads, crying "How shall we go home and see our children die in hunger? They have got no meat these two days and we have nothing to give them."'

The tragedies of Glencoe, Darien and 'the ill years', made the Scots feel sorry for themselves. They thought, 'Would it not be better to break away from England and become a separate nation again?' When Britain was at war with France in Queen Anne's reign, the English feared that the Scots might choose a king of their own and take France's side. They decided to allow the Scots to have free trade, if they would agree to one Parliament for the whole of Britain.

The Act of Union

The Union of the Parliaments took place in 1707. Although favoured by the Scottish nobles, it was opposed by public opinion in Scotland at the time. It meant the end of the old Scottish Parliament in Edinburgh, where lords, lairds and burgesses had all sat in the same House where, as Andrew Fairservice said in *Rob Roy*, 'they didna need to hae the same blethers twice ower'. Forty-five Members of Parliament were to represent Scotland in the British House of Commons in London, and the Scottish lords were to choose 16 of their number to sit in the House of Lords.

Scottish merchants were free to trade with England and the English colonies. At first, Scottish goods could not compare with English ones, but increasing numbers of cattle were driven into England and sold. The cattle trade brought in money, some of which helped to improve farming and the linen industry. Glasgow merchants could now openly import tobacco from Virginia, and the town prospered.

Both countries were to use the same coins, weights and measures, and their Union was marked by a new flag, putting together the crosses of St George and St Andrew. They agreed that the Protestant house of Hanover would succeed to the throne on the death of Queen Anne, but in religion and law Scotland clung to her old ways. The Kirk remained the established Church in Scotland. Scotland kept its own system of law, which is different from English law. Until recently, all members of an English jury, for example, had to agree, whereas in Scotland a majority verdict was enough. A prisoner in England may be either 'guilty' or 'not guilty' but in Scotland a third verdict of 'not proven' (proved) may also be given.

The two peoples united to form one country, Great Britain, and their political history as separate countries came to an end. After 1707, their politics and relations with other countries became the subject-matter of British history. This does not mean that the Scottish nation ceased to exist. Scotland has its own local dialects, songs, dances, stories, customs and traditions – everything that makes up Scottish culture and makes Scottish people feel 'Scottish'. This feeling lives on. If you watch an international football or rugby match you will soon realise that the feeling of Scottish people for their team, and for their country is very strong.

Visits

The A82 road north to Fort William runs through Glencoe, where the National Trust for Scotland's Visitor Centre has a video on the massacre. Parliament House in Edinburgh (off Parliament Square and close to St Giles), where the old Scottish Parliament met until 1707, is also worth visiting.

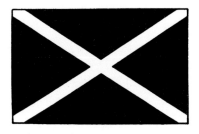

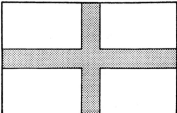

Saltire of Scotland, cross of St George and the Union flag of 1707

29

The Jacobite Risings

Wha the deil hae we gotten for a king,
But a wee, wee German lairdie.

On the death of Queen Anne in 1714, George of Hanover became king of Great Britain. A dull, fat, middle-aged German prince, George was chosen only because he was the Protestant next in line of succession to the throne.

No one in Britain was enthusiastic about his coming. James, the son of James VII, who had been brought up in France, had a more direct claim to the throne, but as a Roman Catholic he was not allowed to be king. James was known as the 'Pretender' – or claimant – to the throne. Later, he came to be called the 'Old Pretender', and his son, Charles, the 'Young Pretender'. In Britain, only the Roman Catholics and some Episcopalians gave James their support, and they were

called Jacobites – 'followers of James'. In the Highlands, many of the clan chiefs remained loyal to him, and defied the government by taking part in the Jacobite risings.

The 'Fifteen

The rebellion in 1715 started badly. Several risings took place, one in the southwest of England, others in Northumberland and Dumfriesshire, but they were on too small a scale and too far away from each other to succeed. In the Highlands, the revolt began under the Earl of Mar. He was nicknamed 'Bobbing John', because he did not join the Jacobite side until he saw that he would gain nothing from supporting George I. When the Pretender's standard was raised 'on the braes of Mar', Braemar in Aberdeenshire, the ball on the top of the flagstaff fell off. The Highlanders regarded this as a warning of defeat.

Mar, whose army had swelled to 10,000 men, marched south and captured Perth. He waited there for the Pretender and the help that had been promised from France. No help came. Louis XIV, the King of France, died before the rising started, and the regent for the infant King Louis XV had no desire to risk war against Britain. The Pretender himself fell ill, and did not arrive until the fighting was over. The delay at Perth was disastrous. Government troops under the Duke

Eilean Donan Castle, held by Spanish troops in the 'Nineteen but blown up and not rebuilt until the early twentieth century

General Wade's military road from near Fort Augustus over the Corrieyairack towards Dalwhinnie, built in 1731 and being restored in 1992, the way the Jacobites came in 1745

of Argyll – 'Red John of the Battles' – arrived to guard the river crossing at Stirling.

Mar sent some men under Mackintosh of Borlum across from Fife to the coast of East Lothian. They might have captured Edinburgh, but instead turned south to join the Jacobites in the north of England, and surrendered after street-fighting in Preston.

Meanwhile at Sheriffmuir, not far from Stirling, the Highlanders and the government army met. Mar, whose troops outnumbered Argyll's by three to one, showed how weak a leader he was by asking the chiefs if they thought he should attack. In the battle, the left wing of each army was routed, neither side being able to claim the victory:

> There's some say that we wan,
> And some say that they wan,
> And some say that nane wan at a', man;

But ae thing I'm sure,
That at Sheriff-muir
A battle there was that I saw, man.

A draw was as serious as a defeat to the Highlanders. The Old Pretender joined them but, pursued by Argyll, they left Perth, crossing the frozen Tay for Dundee and on to Montrose. There the Pretender and Mar embarked on a ship for France. Deserted by their leaders, the clansmen took their best road home.

The 'Nineteen

In 1719, another rising took place with help from Spain. Storms scattered this Spanish Armada, and only two ships carrying 300 Spaniards reached the Isle of Lewis. They crossed to the mainland. Helped only by the Earl of Seaforth's MacKenzies, they were defeated by regular soldiers near what is still known as the 'Spaniards' Pass' in Glenshiel.

The Rule of Walpole (1721–42)

For many years after the 'Nineteen, Robert Walpole was the master of Britain. He is usually considered to have been the first Prime Minister. He took control because George I, who could not speak English, showed so little interest in the business of governing Britain. Since then, while government has still been carried on in the king or queen's name, real power has passed more and more to the Prime Minister.

Under Walpole, the Duke of Argyll and Duncan Forbes of Culloden controlled Scotland. Walpole believed in avoiding trouble, 'letting sleeping dogs lie'. Much smuggling went on at the time; and the people, hating customs duties which kept prices high, were in sympathy with the smugglers. After a smuggler was hanged in Edinburgh, people protested and the City Guard fired on them. Then the crowd lynched Captain Porteous, their captain, by hanging him from a dyer's pole. Stern penalties were imposed on the city, but Walpole wisely reduced them. His leniency kept Edinburgh loyal to the government when the Highlanders invaded the city in 1745.

The early Jacobite risings forced the government to take steps to keep the clansmen in order. An attempt to disarm them failed, because the Highlanders hid their good weapons and handed over rusty ones. General Wade imitated Roman methods by stationing troops in forts – Fort William and two new forts, Fort Augustus and Fort George – and linking them with each other and with the Lowlands by constructing roads. His soldiers built 400 kilometres of roads, and 40 stone bridges including the graceful five-arched bridge over the Tay at Aberfeldy. While they were doing this work, the men received extra money every day to

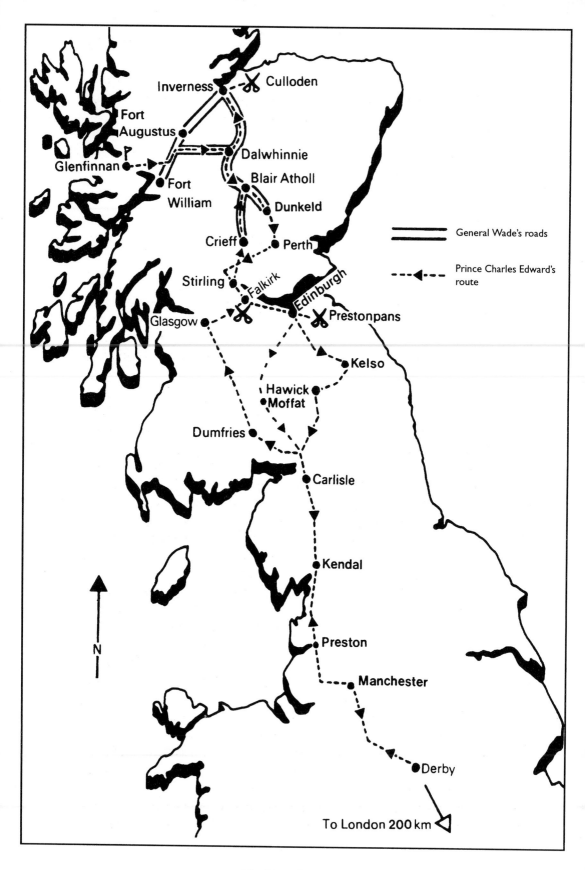

The 'Forty-five rising

supply themselves with food and shelter. Their roads, bordered in places by huge stones to show the direction in the snow, did much to open up the Highlands.

The Highlanders did not welcome the new roads the soldiers built. Used to hill-tracks, they found the gravel surface sore on their feet and for the first time their ponies needed to be shod. Highlanders at least did not agree with the famous lines on Wade and his roads:

> If you'd seen these roads before they were made
> You'd hold up your hands and bless General Wade.

The 'Forty-five

In the 1740s, while Britain was at war on the Continent, Scotland was in an orderly state. In August 1745, Prince Charles Edward, the son of the Old Pretender, arrived in the west Highlands from France with only seven companions. Some chiefs, though loyal to 'the king o'er the water', thought that a Highland rising now without French help was a forlorn hope. Some clansmen had to be forced to join the Prince's army by chiefs who threatened to burn their houses down. Duncan Forbes of Culloden managed to prevent several clans, including the MacKenzies, the MacLeods of Skye and some of the MacDonalds, from helping the Prince.

At Glenfinnan an army of MacDonalds and Camerons raised the standard of rebellion and swept through the Highlands gathering support. They were joined in Perthshire by the men of Atholl under Lord George Murray, who was to command the whole army in attack and retreat. He provided each man with a bag of oatmeal for the journey. He led them through Stirling to Edinburgh, which the Highlanders captured without difficulty by slipping in by the Netherbow Port during the night. The Prince proclaimed his father king at the Mercat Cross. He set up his court at Holyrood Palace where his charm and good looks won the hearts of the ladies, who took to wearing the 'white cockade' – the Jacobite emblem. But the men remained aloof: they would not risk their necks or their lands for a Catholic prince.

Government troops under Sir John Cope were rushed south from the Highlands. At Prestonpans they camped, feeling secure behind a bog which was said to be impassable. In an early morning attack, the Highlanders crossed the bog and overwhelmed them. This victory – commemorated in the famous tune *Hey! Johnnie Cope are ye waukin [awake] yet?* – made Prince Charles supreme in Scotland.

Instead of striking southwards immediately, the Prince remained in Edinburgh, waiting for more men to arrive from the Highlands. This delay, which lasted six weeks, gave the government time to rush troops back from Europe. To avoid meeting them the Highlanders marched on Carlisle and advanced through the north-west of England. They captured Carlisle, Kendal, Preston and Manchester, but without French help almost none of the Lancashire Catholics would join the Prince. Jacobitism in England was dead. The Highlanders were an army of foreigners in a strange land. Finally, at Derby, with the days turning to winter and government armies closing in, the Highland chiefs decided to return home.

They were about 200 kilometres from London, and the capital was in a panic. Would they, as Prince Charles wished, risk their 5,000 clansmen in desperate battle against three government armies totalling 30,000 men? Withdrawal was probably the only sensible course. With the enemy on their heels, the Highlanders turned back. They outpaced their rivals and, with Lord George Murray gallantly covering the retreat, they reached Carlisle, then Glasgow in safety. Such was the condition of the Highlanders when they reached Glasgow that the burgesses were forced to supply them with new clothes – each man received a shirt, stockings, a coat, a bonnet and a pair of shoes.

Culloden

At Falkirk (1746) the clansmen drove off the enemy dragoons at the point of the sword, but they did not follow up their victory. Once they were back in the Highlands, the leaders felt they could hold out, and might return to the attack if more men joined them and if France sent over troops to help. The Highland army

British infantry meeting the Highland charge at Culloden (by David Morier.
The Royal Collection © Her Majesty The Queen)

reached Inverness, but many of the men went home. Meanwhile, a strong force of government troops under George II's son, the Duke of Cumberland, was advancing on Inverness from the east. The Highlanders tried to make a night attack on their camp at Nairn but, weak from lack of food, they failed to reach it before daybreak.

Later that day, on Culloden Moor (1746), the artillery and bayonets of Cumberland's men broke the ranks of the Highlanders who, retreating in the direction of Inverness, were given 'no quarter' by 'Geordie's Wullie', the Duke of Cumberland. Their rebellion was over. The Prince escaped to Skye with the help of Flora MacDonald, and 'safely o'er the friendly main' to France.

Did the Jacobites really have any chance? In 'Bonnie Prince Charlie' they had a more dashing leader than his father, but he was a romantic figure rather than a practical commander of men. He did not work in harmony with Lord George Murray, his ablest general. The march of the Highlanders from Glenfinnan to Derby and back to Culloden is one of the outstanding feats of endurance in history, but the attempt to put a Catholic Stewart back on the throne of Britain, coming so late, appealed to few people outside the Highlands of Scotland.

Visits

Places of Jacobite interest to visit are the Palace of Holyrood in Edinburgh; Culloden (east off the A9 near Inverness) for the scene and the story of the battle, and Fort George (near Inverness airport), which was built to keep the Highlanders quiet after it, the finest Hanoverian fort in Britain.

TOP: *Prince Charles Edward Stuart (miniature) wearing the 'white cockade' (by kind permission of Inverness Museum and Art Gallery)*

BOTTOM: *Flora MacDonald (detail from a painting by Richard Wilson. Courtesy of the Scottish National Portrait Gallery)*

30

The Highlands after the 'Forty-five

The survivors of Culloden returned to their homes in the glens, but the Highlands would never be the same again. Alarmed that the Jacobites had won support chiefly in the Gaelic-speaking north, the government determined to act.

A stricter Disarming Act in 1746 prevented the Highlanders from carrying weapons in public, a custom which had died out in the south, and laid down heavy punishments for hiding them. Plaids, kilts, trews (trousers) and outer coats of tartan were not to be worn. This was the law until 1782. So the kilt was 'ta'en off the Hielandman'. Even the bagpipes were banned as instruments of war!

Winding wool, spinning and carding in Skye in the nineteenth century
(by courtesy of Edinburgh City Libraries)

Highland Regiments

It was the Elder Pitt, as Prime Minister, who made it possible for the Highlanders to fight on the side of the government. The earliest regiment, the Black Watch, which dressed in dark tartan, had been raised before the 'Forty-five to prevent cattle-stealing. Pitt, however, made the proud claim:

> I sought for merit wherever it was to be found. It is my boast that I was the first minister who looked for it and found it in the mountains of the north. I called it forth and drew into your service a hardy and intrepid [brave] race of men . . . These men in the last war [the Seven Years' War] were brought to combat on your side; they served with fidelity [faithfulness] as they fought with valour [courage], and conquered for you in every part of the world.

The early regiments were named after the men who raised them, for example, 'Montgomery's Highlanders' and 'Fraser's Highlanders'. Among the regiments formed by 1800 were the Highland Light Infantry, the Seaforth Highlanders, the Gordons, the Camerons, the Argylls and the Sutherland Highlanders, which along with the Black Watch justified Pitt's confidence in their value to Great Britain. These regiments continued to wear the tartan, and carried on the tradition of playing the bagpipes.

Treatment of Chiefs and People

The government seized the estates of the Jacobite leaders, but gathering in the rents proved no easy matter. When a collector in Lochaber sent his men to seize the belongings of those who refused to pay, the tenants threatened that 'they would beat out their brains'. Later that collector, Colin Campbell of Glenure, was shot. This, the 'Appin Murder', is described in Robert Louis Stevenson's *Kidnapped*.

The commissioners who ran the estates had £5,000 a year to spend on improvements. Some boys from Perthshire were sent south to learn Lowland ways of farming, while a few were trained as weavers, flax-dressers, blacksmiths or cartwrights, and were supplied with tools to practise their crafts in their own districts. Many new roads were made in these estates and 80 bridges were built, including the fine bridge over the Tay at Perth, still carrying traffic today.

For many years the Society in Scotland for Propagating Christian Knowledge had been sending its schoolmasters into the Highlands to teach the reading and writing of English, not Gaelic, in an attempt to make the Highlanders more like the people in the rest of Britain. They told them, too, about the wider world beyond the Highlands, and many young men left their native glens as time went on. The commissioners also started spinning schools, to teach girls to spin using the smaller spinning wheel, and gave them wheels of their own.

The government also broke the power of noblemen and chiefs. For centuries previously, these men had had wide powers over the people under them. They could judge them in their courts and sentence them, and for theft and murder the punishment was death.

In 1747 these 'heritable jurisdictions', as they were called, were abolished. Instead the Highlanders would be judged by sheriffs who were qualified men of law. Chiefs lost their absolute power over their men, and took less interest in their affairs. The generous grants of land a chief used to give to his relatives, the tacksmen, were ended, because there was no longer any need to maintain these men as a privileged class of warriors. The chief was no longer 'the father of his clan'. As an old chief said afterwards, 'In my youth men asked how many men a chief had on his lands; now they ask how many black cattle he has'. The chief became a landlord and a farmer, and the clan system continued to decay.

Farming

The number of people living in the Highlands increased considerably in the years after Culloden. Good farming land was scarce and rents were raised. The people were poor, but potatoes, a new crop, helped to keep them alive. Supposed to have been brought to England from South America by Sir Walter Raleigh, potatoes

Planting potatoes in 1890, the man is using a caschrom
(by courtesy of Edinburgh City Libraries)

*Highland drovers and cattle (detail from a drawing by James Howe.
Courtesy of the National Gallery of Scotland)*

began to be grown in Scotland in the eighteenth century. When he saw how the poor people lived on them in Ireland, Clanranald brought some to South Uist in 1743 and showed his tenants how to grow them. When the crop was gathered, the men dumped it at Clanranald's gate. He could force them to grow potatoes but they were determined not to eat them. But soon people all over the Highlands and Islands were growing and eating potatoes. They were eaten at every meal and, it is said, formed four-fifths of the food of the people living in the Hebrides in 1811.

The only time many Highlanders handled any money was when they sold some cattle. Drovers with their dogs collected the cattle and drove them south to be sold at the Tryst at Falkirk. This was a convenient centre and nearer to England than Crieff, and it became the main market for cattle. On the long journey into England, the cattle needed to be shod. One blacksmith at Boroughbridge in Yorkshire made 30,000 shoes for them each autumn. To avoid paying tolls on main roads the drovers used rough tracks called 'drove roads', which can still be identified in many districts. The animals lost weight on the journey, but were fattened up on pastures in the south for the London market. In 1794 they were selling at Falkirk for £4 a head.

The Highland Clearances

Then landlords learned they could make more money by letting the land to big sheep-farmers, and blackface sheep were brought in with their shepherds from the south. These were hardy sheep which could be left out on the hills in all weathers. Cheviot sheep came next. Their wool was much finer and was worth a lot more but the sheep had to be brought down from the hills to shelter in the glens in winter and feed on hay and turnips.

To make room for them the landlords took away the land from many people and cleared them out of their homes. We can often see the ruins of deserted houses in the Highlands today, as well as the remains of many other buildings which were once the homes, store-houses, animal shelters, grain-drying kilns and corn mill of the people in a whole village. In 1811, 20 families were living in such a village, called Grummore, beside Loch Naver in the north of Sutherland. The model below is a careful reconstruction of how it must have looked then. Its people were among those who were ordered 'man, women and child . . . from the heights of Farr to the mouth of the Naver, on one day, to quit their tenements [holdings] and go . . . many of them knew not whither.' This was 1819. The order was enforced without pity; the houses were set on fire and tenants dashed about madly, trying to save their relatives, their cattle and their belongings. They made their way to the coast to live on little strips of land called 'crofts', where they had to build houses for themselves and try to make a living by fishing. Some moved south to industrial towns in the Lowlands, while others began to think of emigrating to America. Sheep graze among the ruins of this settlement today but no one lives there any more. Not all clearances were carried out as ruthlessly as this one, but they destroyed any feeling of respect a tenant might have had for his landlord.

Scale model of Grummore before 1819, its buildings restored and patches
of land cultivated (photograph by Alan Beattie)

31

The Improving Farmers

As far as farming was concerned, much of Scotland in the early eighteenth century had changed little since the Middle Ages. The land had a bare look. There were few trees, because the people had cut them down for building and for burning as fuel, and had not replanted. Even near towns the ploughed land lay open. Beside the rivers, where the land was marshy and the soil sour, nothing would grow.

Although some farmers had compact farms of their own, and for almost a century had owned their fields, most people still farmed on the old runrig system, described on page 65. Around their touns or hamlets they grew oats and barley on their scattered rigs in the infield, and grazed their cattle on most of the outfield. In some districts flax, peas, and beans were important crops, while along the drier east coast – in East Lothian, for example – wheat was grown. Yields of corn were never high, and farmers had learned not to expect much. According to an old Scots saying, the harvest was divided into three parts:

> Ane to saw [sow], ane to gnaw [eat]
> And ane to pay the laird witha'.

The position of Scottish farming is very different today. Scottish sheep and beef cattle have a high reputation. The countryside looks prosperous. Crops flourish, aided by skilful crop-rotation and new fertilisers, in fields divided by hedges and belts of trees. Farmhouses and outbuildings are well built. Machines like the tractor and combine-harvester do the work of many men and animals quickly and efficiently. In the last 300 years, methods of farming have been improved and the face of the countryside has completely altered. A complete change is known as a 'revolution', and to these changes we give the name The Agricultural Revolution.

The Agricultural Revolution in England

How did it start? After the Union with England in 1707, the Scottish lairds learned that some English methods of farming were better than their own and began to copy them. In the course of the eighteenth century, England abandoned her traditional open field system by which every tenant cultivated scattered strips but grew the same crops. Landlords divided up their estates and gave each tenant a large compact parcel of land where he could grow what he wanted. Broadly speaking, England led at the start of the Agricultural Revolution and Scotland followed.

In England, Jethro Tull invented the seed-drill, and was the pioneer of sowing seed in drills or rows. His invention was especially useful for growing turnips. Lord Townshend – nicknamed 'Turnip' – saw the value of this crop to the farmer. In Norfolk he found that turnips cleared the ground and that grain grown in a field a year after a crop of turnips, gave a heavier yield. Besides, the turnip proved to be the foundation of animal farming. It was ideal for fattening cattle, and when it was fed to cattle in winter farmers did not need to kill so many animals the following autumn.

The Agricultural Revolution in Scotland

We can see the changes in Scottish farming best by studying carefully what happened on a single estate.

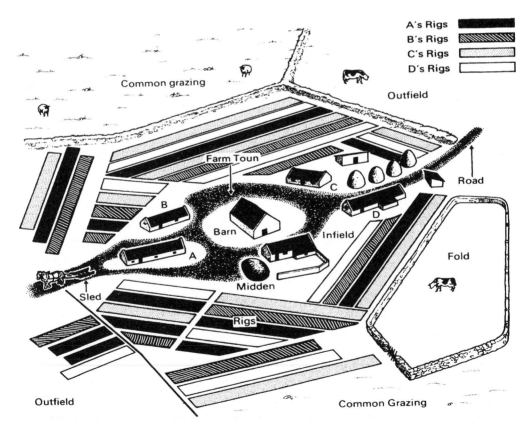

Runrig farming

Archibald Grant's father bought the estate of Monymusk in Aberdeenshire. Ten thousand acres (about 4,000 hectares) of poorly cultivated land, it has all the faults of the old system of farming in Scotland. As he rides over the estate with Archibald, he stops from time to time and shakes his head in despair.

'Look, Archie, look at this wilderness – stones lying about everywhere, weeds choking the barley crop, and these scraggy cows eating the young oat shoots. See all the land that isn't cultivated at all, there between those rigs, there on the hill and down there, all that bog land. There's hardly a full-grown tree on the whole estate, not a cart in the place, not even a decent road. Och, I should never have bought this place! These poor creatures in their miserable huts down there – surely they must see that they'll never be any better off if they keep on farming like this.' He grunts in disgust.

They ride on to the farm toun of Todlachie.

'Hey there, Simpson,' he shouts to one of the tenants – 'why don't you leave a bit of your land fallow every year?'

'Fallow, sir? I dinna ken what ye mean.'

'Well, don't sow corn in all your infield land every year. Let a bit of it grow nothing for a year; let it have a rest, like you do when you go to sleep at night, and it will give you a bigger crop next year.'

'Och, we couldna' dae that, sir. It wad be a waste o' ground. Onyway, we've aye done it this way.'

As the riders turn away towards Monymusk, the laird mutters under his breath. 'They've aye done it this way – they've aye done it this way. Will they never learn?' He pulls up his horse.

'Archie, there's no use telling them what to do. We'll have to show them. No, *you'll* have to show them – I'm too busy in my courtroom in Edinburgh. You'll have to improve this estate until they see the benefits of better ways, and then they'll change.'

Archibald Grant set to work with a will. Not only did he improve the land, he also left records of the changes he made. For example, in 1758 he noted that 85,100 fir trees were added to his plantations. He planted millions of trees in his lifetime. The timber was valuable for making implements, building houses, and making fences. It was also an investment. This was the view expressed by the Laird of Dumbiedykes in Sir Walter Scott's *Heart of Midlothian*, when he told his son:

> Jock, when ye hae naething else to do, ye may be aye sticking in a tree; it will aye be growing, Jock, when ye're sleeping.

On the copy of part of General Roy's map (*see* page 164) we can see where Archibald Grant grew trees and the drystone dykes that were built round the kind of fields we recognise today. The dykes kept animals out of the growing crops. Labourers also dug drains in marshy ground and threw loose stones into the bottom of them so that water seeped through and left the land drier. This gave him

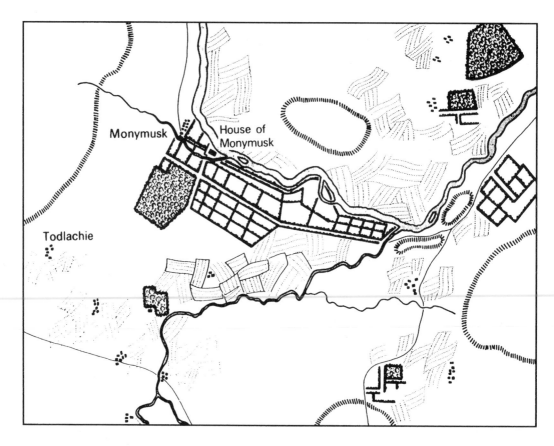

*Monymusk beside the River Don in Aberdeenshire, from an early map by
General Roy showing signs of Archibald Grant's improvements*

more land suitable for growing crops. He sowed grass as a crop and made hay as
winter feed for animals. He was one of the first to plant potatoes. Growing turnips
in drills, he worked out a scientific rotation of crops: barley and clover the first
year, turnips the next, then oats and then peas. In all these ways he was making far
better use of his land.

The map also shows that some tenants, at Todlachie for example, were still
farming in the old way. Archibald Grant tried hard to persuade them to follow his
example. Constantly he rode round his estate giving advice. For those who would
not take it he had little sympathy. 'As to your poor living,' he told them, 'I am sorry
for it but it is your own fault.' He encouraged keen tenants to exchange their
scattered rigs with one another until each had all his land together. Where farms
were too small, he joined two farms together and gave one of the farmers a new
holding on higher land, which was rent-free at first. Previously, tenants had feared
that the laird might take away their land, but Archibald Grant gave them long
leases, or use of their land – say, for 21 years – to let them reap the benefit of the

improvements they made. Usually he asked for higher rents and insisted that tenants sow turnips, potatoes and grass. One tenant was instructed that he must not 'leave a stone in said Enclosure which 3 men can roll to the dyke or 4 men can carry on a Barrow'.

The changes at Monymusk improved the estate and made the farms produce far more. But some men did not benefit: they lost their land and left the district. Others took up new jobs as gardeners, tree-planters and labourers, while craftsmen like blacksmiths and wheelwrights found their services in constant demand.

Changes like these were taking place all over Lowland Scotland, and most districts could boast an improving laird. Landlords and the enterprising tenants who imitated them turned agriculture into a flourishing industry. They still needed many workers to cultivate the land. Most of the work was done by labourers who had no land of their own, in return for their keep and a small wage.

Animal Breeding

Through careful breeding and winter feeding, cattle and sheep in the last 200 years have increased in size and improved in quality. Galloway cattle, for example, used to weigh less than half their present-day weight. Many animals are now pure-bred, and breeders are prepared to pay high prices for pedigree stock. The Aberdeen-

Clydesdales at the Highland Show

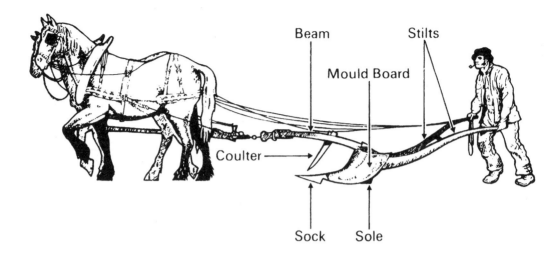

Beam   Stilts

Mould Board

Coulter

Sock   Sole

Small's swing plough

Angus breed of cattle was founded by Hugh Watson of Keillor near Coupar Angus, and is renowned for its high quality beef. Galloways are also famous beef cattle, and Ayrshire cows give high yields of good quality milk. Among horses the powerful Scottish Clydesdale became very popular as a cart-horse and a plough-horse.

Scottish Farming Inventors

When the Agricultural Revolution was under way, James Small, a Berwickshire tool-maker, invented a swing-plough. This type of plough had no wheels and could be lifted out of the furrow by pressing down the handles. Its mould-board was curved so that it turned the soil over more easily. Most important of all, it could be pulled by two horses instead of a team of eight or ten oxen. It was in use in most Lowland counties by 1800.

Another Scot, Andrew Meikle, invented a threshing machine. Previously, labourers had to hit the heads of the grain with flails to separate the grain from the stalks. His machine, driven by horses or water power, saved time and labour.

Cutting corn with a sickle or scythe had always been a wearisome job, requiring many workers. Patrick Bell, a Scottish minister, invented a reaping machine in 1827. In America the McCormicks improved on it with their harvester which was used to cut the great grain crops on the prairies.

Since then farming has become a mechanised industry. The outstanding example is the tractor, which has almost completely displaced the horse. With machines, farmers can now produce far more food with less labour. The drift of workers from the country to the town which began then is still going on.

Boom and Slump in Farming

The Corn Law in 1815 encouraged British farmers to grow grain by keeping foreign grain out. The price of bread was always high. In 1846, after a potato famine in Ireland and poor grain crops here, Sir Robert Peel repealed the Corn Laws. Foreign grain was brought in to relieve the starving, and prices fell. British farmers did not suffer immediately from this foreign competition, because the number of people in the country was rising all the time and so was the demand for bread. By the 1870s, however, wheat grown on the virgin soils of Canada and the USA began to be imported in new iron-hulled cargo ships, in such bulk that British farmers could not compete. Wheat prices fell by nearly a half from 1870 to 1913. Farmers here planted less grain, and some turned their land over to pasture for animals. After 1875 the great depression in farming set in. Many farmers could not make ends meet, and gave up their farms. Farm buildings and cottages all over the country fell into ruins.

In 1914, with the beginning of the First World War, farming recovered, because in wartime it was vital to produce as much food as possible at home. Even so people in Britain came close to starvation. In 1917 German submarines went to sea with orders to attack any ship, enemy or neutral, trading with Britain. Nearly a million tonnes of shipping were sunk in April alone, and Britain had only

Border landscape at harvest-time

enough food left to last six weeks. By adopting the convoy system when merchant ships sailed together in groups escorted by warships of the Royal Navy, fewer ships were lost. At home farmers were told what crops to grow and food was rationed to share it out equally. The situation in the Second World War (1939–45) was similar and after it the government continued to encourage farmers to grow as much of the food as possible that the British people needed.

When Britain joined the European Economic Community in 1972, however, she became part of a much bigger market. Support payments from the Community persuaded farmers to grow more of certain crops, yellow fields of oilseed rape, for example, for the production of cooking oil, and less of others, such as wheat and barley. The days of Scottish farmers producing all they can from their land appear to be over.

Some Farming Pioneers

IMPROVER	DISTRICT	IMPROVEMENT
John Cockburn of Ormiston	East Lothian	enclosures, vegetables
Lord Kames	Berwickshire and Perthshire	potatoes, grasses
William Craig of Arbigland	Kirkcudbright	land clearance
Robert Maxwell of Arkland	Dumfriesshire	Secretary of 'Society of Improvers'
William Dawson of Frogden	Roxburghshire	turnips, animal breeding
Sir John Sinclair	Caithness	enclosures, started the *Statistical Account of Scotland*
Robert Barclay of Urie	Kincardine	drainage, crop rotation

Visits

If you are near Edinburgh in June, visit The Royal Highland Show at Ingliston, close to the airport. This is the place to see the finest farm animals and machinery, and demonstrations of rural crafts, such as shoeing horses and shearing sheep. The excellent agricultural museum there is full of material on life and work on Scottish farms in the past.

32

Edinburgh in the Eighteenth Century and Today

If you had been able to visit Edinburgh in the early eighteenth century you would have found it an overcrowded town. Its main street ran down the ridge, now called 'The Royal Mile', from the Castle on the west to the Palace of Holyrood on the east. The other main street, the Cowgate, lay to the south and was linked with it by narrow wynds. On the north side, where the train tracks run today, the Nor' Loch was still an undrained swamp, and beyond were green fields and trees, where Princes Street and all the streets to the north of it were later to be built.

The town was small – too small in 1707 to house its population of 40,000 except in tenements called 'lands', like Gladstone's Land in the Lawnmarket. This belonged to Thomas Gladstone, a merchant, but four other families bought flats in it. Sometimes 12 storeys high, these 'lands' were like early skyscrapers. You entered a house either by climbing up the stairs at the front, called the 'forestairs', or by going up a close to the common stair. As the population grew, other houses were built up the close, in what had once been the long gardens of the houses on the street.

Farther down the street the Canongate, which had been a separate burgh until 1636, contained the town houses of many Scottish lords. Not so tall or crowded as those up nearer the Castle, these houses were set in fine gardens. An Englishman said the garden of Moray House, now a College of Education, was equal to 'those of warmer countries and perhaps even of England itself', (*see* the plan on page 68).

In the lofty lands the poorest folk lived in the cellars, tradesmen in the attics, with clerks, merchants, doctors, lawyers and an occasional noble lord in between. All classes of people lived up the same stair. Living together like this they all spoke 'the braid Scots'. You could tell that a man was a gentleman by his clothes, not by the way he spoke.

Even the houses of well-off people were not large. Mr Bruce, a lawyer, had a flat in Forester's Wynd off the Lawnmarket for £15 a year. It had three rooms and a kitchen. One room – known as the parlour – was 'my lady's', another was a study, and the third a bedroom. The children slept in the study, on beds which were put up every night and removed in the morning. The maid slept in the kitchen under the dresser, and the serving man slept out. Mr Bruce slept in a 'press-bed' curtained off from the rest of the room.

In the Street

The town woke early. Shops were open at seven and scholars were already off to school. Cows were driven off to graze on the Burgh Muir. Pigs left their sties under the forestairs and wandered about the street. Morning washing appeared on

Gladstone's Land with its arches and forestairs

poles stuck out from the windows. People were out and about: carters brought food into the town, milkmaids sold buttermilk from barrels slung over the saddle of a horse, fishwives trudged into town carrying heavy creels of their backs. They cried their wares. Women gossiped and bargained, men quarrelled, children played. It was a noisy, boisterous town.

Men were off to their places of business: the judge to his court, the merchant to his shop, the craftsman to his workshop. The Luckenbooths, the lock-up shops near St Giles, were opened up for the day in the most crowded part of the street. In the Lawnmarket soldiers from the Castle wandered about among the stalls of food and cloth, looking at everything but buying little. Since wages were low, housewives did not think that food was cheap, but today we tend to look with envy at the prices they paid. Chickens cost from 8d. to 1s. (3p to 5p) a pair, beef from 2½d. to 4½d. a pound (2p to 4p per kilo), buttermilk 1d. (½p) a Scots pint (equal to three English pints), coal from 5d. to 6d. (2p to 2½p) per bag. But China tea cost 30s. a pound (£3.30 per kilo) in the reign of Queen Anne. Only those who were rich enough could follow the new fashion of tea-drinking, and water had to be paid for. The water-caddies charged 1d. (½p) a barrel for the water they carried from the public wells.

People were dirty, houses were dirty, the street was dirty. Soap was not yet in common use. Early in the century, men trimmed their beards on Saturday to look clean on Sunday. Few people cleaned their teeth, because it was thought to cause rheumatics in the teeth. Houses to which water had to be carried attracted vermin, and Professor Reid rejoiced because he had a house free from bugs. There was no piped drainage, and at ten o'clock each night, with a cry of 'Gardyloo!' ('mind the water'), housewives and maids threw their filth and dirty water out into the street. Passers-by roared 'Haud yer hand!' and rushed to safety.

The Athens of the North

After 1707 the government of Scotland was not in Edinburgh any more, but the town still saw its share of historical events. The Porteous Riots took place there, as we have seen (*see* page 151). The city was captured by the Jacobites in 1745. Prince Charles Edward lived in Holyrood and proclaimed his father king (although the garrison held the Castle against him). Later, Edinburgh became a great European centre of learning and the arts. Its university teachers were famous, and so many thinkers and writers lived there that people regarded the city as the capital of learning in Europe, as Athens had been in the time of Plato in the fourth century BC. They called Edinburgh 'The Athens of the North'.

No one has ever been able to explain why certain generations in history have produced so many great men living at the same time, as was the case with the masters of painting and sculpture in Italy during the Renaissance, for example. The rapid growth in the numbers attending Edinburgh University, doubling in the

Procession in the Lawnmarket, Edinburgh, about 1850
(by courtesy of Edinburgh City Libraries)

20 years after 1763, probably contributed, along with the rising professional classes, such as doctors and lawyers, who could afford to buy books.

The recognised leader in learning in eighteenth century Edinburgh was David Hume, author of the *Treatise on Human Nature* and the *History of England*. Prominent also stood Kirkcaldy's most famous son, Adam Smith, who wrote the masterpiece, *The Wealth of Nations*. In it he showed that nations prospered by trading freely with one another. John Home, a minister who wrote the play *Douglas*, started a craze for theatre-going which affected even ministers of the Kirk when the General Assembly was being held. Allan Ramsay, besides being a bookseller who started the first circulating library in his shop in the Luckenbooths, was an outstanding poet who wrote *The Gentle Shepherd*. Robert Fergusson, Edinburgh's own poet who died tragically at the age of 24, was recognised by Robert Burns as a master.

There was Burns himself, the Ayrshire farmer whose poems when they were first published in Kilmarnock were eagerly bought even by dairymaids and ploughmen. In his poems they saw people like themselves and their neighbours pictured in language which they could understand and enjoy. When Burns arrived in Edinburgh he was welcomed by the nobility and the scholars, and found himself famous. Among those who met him was the young Walter Scott, who was to make a name for himself as the collector of old ballads and the author of many historical novels.

Two women became famous for their songs. In reply to a challenge Jean Elliot wrote *The Liltin'*, another version of *The Flowers of the Forest*, describing the Borders after the battle of Flodden. Lady Nairne ranks second only to Burns as a writer of songs. Do you know *Wi' a Hunder Pipers, Will Ye No Come Back Again?* and *Caller Herrin'*? They are all by Lady Nairne.

Tam o' Shanter and Souter Johnnie, characters in Burns' Tam o' Shanter

The New Town

Edinburgh was crowded and had to expand. It expanded first towards the south, to George Square, in the 1760s. Then the North Bridge was built, and in 1767 James Craig, the architect, made a bold plan for the 'New Town' north of the Nor' Loch, but men had to be encouraged to build there. For example, the first house at the east end of Princes Street was declared free of rates for all time. Princes Street began as a street of houses looking over the drained Nor' Loch to the tall tenements of the Old Town. North of Princes Street, broad new streets were laid out, their names showing respect for the royal family – George Street, Queen Street, Frederick Street, Hanover Street.

The well-planned houses in the classical style were far more comfortable and dignified and airy than the cramped flats in the Old Town. The lords and the merchants, the lawyers and the professors moved over to the New Town, leaving their houses in the High Street to poorer people. For example, in 1783 one judge's house had become the home of a French teacher and the house of another had passed to a 'rouping-wife' or saleswoman of old furniture. The High Street ceased to be the centre of Edinburgh, and in the early twentieth century its tenements decayed into slums.

Edinburgh Today

The city has been growing ever since. With the chief government offices for Scotland situated in Edinburgh, along with the headquarters of the Scottish banks and insurance companies, a large number of people are office workers. It is a famous centre of law and also of learning, with many schools and colleges and now three universities, The University of Edinburgh, Heriot-Watt University and Napier University. Old-established industries include brewing and printing – *The Scotsman* newspaper, for example, dates back to 1817. More recent enterprises manufacture defence and security systems, and medical equipment as well as beds and biscuits. Far more people work in shops and hotels, however, because Edinburgh is a centre for shopping and entertainment, and popular with tourists.

Many of the bigger houses in the New Town were turned into shops or offices. More people arrived and an even newer town had to be built. In some districts stone-built tenements arose, in others detached villas built of stone and later of brick. While old houses were decaying, the standards expected in housing were being raised, and more and more new houses were required. During the 1920s and 1930s about 2,000 houses were being built every year, half of them council houses and half private villas and bungalows. In other words, a new built-up area equal in size to the Old Town of 1750 was being added to Edinburgh *every year*.

Edinburgh spread outwards and towns such as the port of Leith and South Queensferry and former villages like Corstorphine and Liberton are now inside the modern city. In the 1990s the pace of building slowed and now some people have difficulty in finding a place to live.

The shortage of jobs is more serious. Opportunities in the future are likely to arise either in new research centres, like the Heriot-Watt University Science Park, or by building on existing strengths, such as financial management. In terms of the value of the stocks and shares fund managers in the city hold, Edinburgh is the second biggest financial centre in the U.K. and the fourth biggest in the European Economic Community.

Edinburgh is also the centre where the European summit was held in December 1992 and where the Commonwealth heads of government met in October 1997, and the building of the Edinburgh International Conference Centre makes it a competitor with other European cities. Its International Festival of Music and Drama and the Festival Fringe are both well established and attract thousands of visitors to the city every year.

Seeing the City

The best place from which to view the city is either the Castle Esplanade or the Radical Road under Arthur's Seat in Holyrood Park, or you can enjoy the sights from one of the open-topped buses which tour the city (most operate from Waverley Bridge, close to the railway station).

To explore the Old Town it is best to walk along the High Street, downhill from the Castle to the Palace of Holyroodhouse.

To contrast life in the Old Town with the New, visit Gladstone's Land, a well-preserved seventeenth century building situated in the Lawnmarket, then the eighteenth-century Georgian House in Charlotte Square. Both are authentically furnished. The Old Town and the New Town are now recognised as a World Heritage Site.

Charlotte Square, designed by Robert Adam, at the west end of
George Street in the New Town

33

The Industrial Revolution: Cloth

New Ways of Making Things

During the eighteenth century Scotland began to prosper. Methods of farming were much better. Trade with England expanded and Scottish merchants were beginning to buy and sell in new markets in the colonies. The population was rising, and old towns and quiet villages were growing steadily. Later in the century a more fundamental change began, not sudden but prolonged, for it is still going on – a change we call The Industrial Revolution.

Ways of making things were changed. Old tools and machines worked by hand gave way to faster, complicated machinery, driven by water or steam power. Cottage industries suffered because they could not compete with the new machines, and men who had worked at home had to give in and go and work for wages in factories.

The new machines cost too much for the average worker to buy. An employer provided them in the factory he built near a source of energy. Factories using water power were set up beside swift-flowing streams. Later, when James Watt's improved steam engine could drive machinery, many factories were built on coalfields where the fuel was. Workers all worked the same long hours, at the pace of their machines.

New towns sprang up and old ones expanded on the coalfields. As population increased at a time of agricultural change, people left the countryside to look for work in towns nearby. Many became factory workers living in towns.

Manufacturers produced far more than their local customers could buy, in the hope that they would sell all they could make. Selling became important and they took steps to sell the rest farther away. In towns many new shops were opened which stocked a wide range of goods from different manufacturers.

Improvements were made in transport to bring in new raw materials and to move goods away from the factories to the markets where they would be sold.

Linen

Linen is made from the fibres inside the stalk of the flax plant but a great deal has to be done to the flax before it is ready for spinning. First, it is left to steep in water to help to rot its vegetable skin. When it has dried, the next stage is 'scutching', that is, beating it with mallets to get rid of the skin, and finally comes 'heckling', which is when the fibres are combed out.

The natural colour of linen is pale yellowish-brown but people liked linen cloth to be white. On the next page, the women are bleaching pieces of cloth on the Calton Hill in Edinburgh. They soak the cloth in buttermilk in the tubs and then expose it to the sun. The watering-cans are for watering the cloth so that it does not dry with the milk in it. This process of souring the cloth with milk and then watering it was done over and over again until the cloth became white.

The Board of Trustees for Manufactures brought in skilled spinners and weavers from abroad to try to improve the quality of the cloth, and also set up spinning schools to teach girls to spin. The Board made the preparation of flax for

The steam engine, work-horse of the Industrial Revolution, in a Selkirk woollen mill
(photograph by John R. Hume, Historic Scotland)

spinning easier by building many lint mills in central Scotland and the north-east. Spinning and weaving, however, were still carried on in people's homes. Money was also provided for bleachfields at Dumbarton, Glasgow, Edinburgh, Cupar, Aberdeen and Perth.

Later on, bleaching was speeded up by using sulphuric acid and then Charles Mackintosh, of waterproof fame, invented bleaching powder (chloride of lime). This was a great improvement: it bleached quickly, it was easy to transport and, mass-produced at the St Rollox Chemical Works in Glasgow, it became very cheap.

Fife and Angus, facing the Baltic where most of the flax came from, produced the most linen cloth but it was coarse in quality and cheap in price. Finer linen was produced in Lanarkshire and Renfrewshire. The Glasgow district in 1778 contained 4,000 looms, 500 of them in the village of Anderston alone. Between 1740 and 1800 the amount of linen woven in Scotland increased five-fold to over 21 million metres.

As linen-making became a factory industry, it caused the growth of several of our early industrial towns, such as Paisley, Dundee, Dunfermline and Perth. In spite of competition from cotton, linen was in demand for tablecloths, shirts and sails for many years.

Bleaching linen on the Calton Hill, Edinburgh, in 1825
(by courtesy of Edinburgh City Libraries)

New Lanark

The Coming of Cotton

Linen met a serious rival in cotton. Already in England the cotton industry was forging ahead in the dampness of Lancashire. Inventions like Richard Arkwright's water frame and Samuel Crompton's spinning mule speeded up the production of yarn, and were applied first in the cotton industry. The new machines used up the raw material far more quickly, but the cotton crop could be increased by extending the area where it was grown. It was cheaper to grow than flax, because work in the cotton-fields of America was done by slaves. In America, Eli Whitney's invention, the cotton gin or engine, cleaned cotton easily and made it ready for spinning.

'Why not make cotton cloth in the west of Scotland?' thought David Dale, a Glasgow yarn merchant and banker. 'The atmosphere is damp enough to stop the threads from breaking; the skill of the linen weavers is here already and they can just as easily weave cotton; and besides, Glasgow faces west and can import raw cotton from America.' He consulted Richard Arkwright, and built a factory at New Lanark where he used water power from the Falls of Clyde to drive the spinning frames.

By 1791, 15,000 weavers from Girvan to Stirling were working in their homes for Glasgow manufacturers. The demand for cotton cloth was so great at home and overseas that handloom weavers earned more than ever. Many earned two pounds a week, while some could keep themselves in comfort by working only four days a week. They were well off, and their dress and their bearing as they walked out with their families on a Sunday proved that they knew it.

The weavers' prosperity did not last. The craft they had taken up so keenly as boys in 1800 was not one they would recommend to their grandsons 50 years later. Edmund Cartwright, an English clergyman, had invented a power loom and so weaving became a factory industry. James Watt's improved steam engine supplied the power to drive the machines. Together the steam engine and the power loom hastened the end of weaving at home. The handloom weavers worked longer hours and wove more intricate patterns, but their wages continued to fall until in 1850 they were earning only one-fifth of what weavers earned 50 years before.

Machine-made cotton caused a revolution in people's homes and in dress. The cloth was cheap and reached a far wider public. There were cloths for the table and lace or muslin curtains to adorn the windows. Women wore cotton clothes 'from the muslin cap on the crown of the head to the cotton stockings under the sole of the foot'. The habit of wearing cotton underclothes spread because they were light and cheap and could be changed and washed often.

On the whole no cotton manufacturer in Scotland set out to make everything. Each tried to meet a particular demand. For example, the towns of Darvel, Newmilns and Galston in North Ayrshire specialised in making lace. Johnstone and Paisley became the centres of thread-making, and J. & P. Coats of Paisley is still a well-known name.

The Fashion in Paisley Shawls

As the names of streets like Gauze Street, Cotton Street and Shuttle Street suggest, Paisley owes its expansion to its textile factories. In 1820 there were 7,000 weavers in the town, most of them making Paisley shawls. These were copies of Indian shawls, made from the finest wool. Many artists were employed in Paisley at that time, working out intricate patterns and colour blends to catch the eye. Months of preparation went into the design of a single shawl; it took a week to weave the elaborate pattern. Paisley shawls became the fashion – every woman wanted one. Queen Victoria wore them, and in one order she bought 17 which cost her £91.

The Paisley shawl was so successful that imitators tried to make something like it, not weaving the pattern into the cloth but just printing it on plain cloth. The imitation shawl cost only a quarter of the price. It 'cheapened' the original, fashion changed, and the trade died.

Jute in Dundee

In the 1830s Dundee began to import the fibres of the tall jute crop grown on the Ganges Delta near Calcutta. The fibres made strong coarse yarn suitable for sacking. The industry developed and the town grew rapidly. Carpeting and backings for carpets and linoleum were manufactured there as well as millions of coal-bags, flour-bags and sugar-bags. Faced by competition from other kinds of containers such as plastic bags as well as competition from mills using cheaper labour in India and Pakistan, the number of workers in the jute industry in Dundee has withered away.

Scotch Tweed

Wherever there were sheep, there was weaving of woollen cloth, and warm clothes are essential in Scotland. Two main areas specialised in making woollens, the Borders and the Hillfoot towns like Alloa, Alva, Dollar and Tillicoultry. The Old Statistical Account tells us that in the 1790s blankets and serges made in Alva were worth over £7,000 a year and were sent to Glasgow, Edinburgh and Dundee. The weavers changed to making tartans when tartan shawls and plaids became the fashion.

Galashiels turned from making 'Gala Blues', the tough blue cloth worn by sailors, because of a new fashion. Sir Walter Scott and Lord Brougham helped to make the black-and-white check that Border shepherds wore into fashionable wear for men. Brighter mixtures of colours were introduced, and weavers made a wide range of patterns which merchants and tailors could inspect before ordering large pieces of cloth. This became the system on which many Scottish manufacturers worked, and Scottish woollens became famous for their designs – and their designers.

Generally, woollens were later than cotton in becoming a factory industry, because the supply of local wool was limited. Then fine wool was imported from Germany, and later from Australia and New Zealand. Along the river valleys, mills were erected to house machines like spinning mules and power looms, which had been adapted from the cotton industry.

The name 'tweed' does not refer to the River Tweed where the Border woollen towns are: it was adopted by accident. Some patterns are called 'twills', pronounced 'tweels' in the Borders. In a letter to a London merchant a clerk in Hawick wrote the word 'tweels'. The merchant mis-read it as 'tweeds' and a new name was born. It refers to cloth made not only in the Borders but all over Scotland. Even the woollen cloth the crofters weave in the Hebrides is called Harris tweed.

The Revival of Tartan

By 1782 when the ban on wearing tartan ended, most Highlanders had found that trousers made of thick, dark-coloured cloth were a good protection against the wind and the weather (*see* the man on page 158).

Soldiers in the Highland regiments wore dark tartans. The black, dark blue and dark green of the Black Watch was the basis for other tartans. Its pattern with yellow stripes added became the tartan of the Gordon Highlanders, and with red and white stripes of the Seaforth Highlanders.

By the 1820s old fears of the Jacobites and of Highlanders being rebels had long faded away. In 1822 George IV, the fourth king in a row called George since 1714, became the first of them ever to visit Scotland. The event was stage-managed by Sir Walter Scott, author of *The Waverley Novels* and at a reception at Holyroodhouse the King appeared wearing a kilt of Royal Stewart tartan. This started a craze for tartan.

Messrs Wilson of Bannockburn were the main weavers and they invented a great many new tartans. Not only were there clan tartans, but hunting tartans and dress tartans, ancient tartans with muted colours and tartans even for Border families, such as Scotts and Armstrongs who had no history of wearing tartan. Finally, Queen Victoria (1837–1901), enjoying Balmoral Castle and even furnishing it with tartan, her children wearing kilts and appearing at the Braemar Highland Games in Highland dress, set the royal seal of approval to tartan.

Visits

An outstanding place to visit is Dale and Owen's spinning mills not far from Lanark at New Lanark, now a World Heritage Village, where it is exciting to share in the Annie McLeod Experience.

Balmoral, Queen Victoria's Highland home, the initials 'GR' and 'MR' represent her grandson King George V and Queen Mary 1910–36, grandparents of H.M. Queen Elizabeth 1952–

34

The Industrial Revolution: Iron, Steel and Coal

Iron

Weapons and tools made of iron were brought to Britain by the Celts before the Romans came. We call this the 'Iron Age', which has been going on ever since. It is still true to say that this is an Age of Iron and Steel.

To produce iron, the iron ore it is found in has to be made so hot that the iron melts and runs off. This process, called 'smelting', could be done by burning charcoal along with the ore. Where there were plenty of woods to make charcoal, in Argyll, for example, furnaces were built to produce iron. When wood became scarce in England, however, Abraham Darby of Coalbrookdale in Shropshire found a substitute by using coke, which could be made from the best coal. After his discovery, the new iron works were built on coalfields.

In 1759 the Carron Iron Works at Falkirk was the first to use the coal and iron ore of central Scotland. The skilled workers came from England. Soon they were making farm implements, nails, fire grates and stoves, and guns called 'carronades' for half the armies and navies of Europe. The Duke of Wellington insisted on them

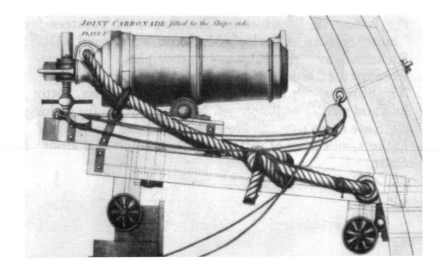

Carronade, the kind used in ships

for his army in the Peninsular War. He wrote: 'I have had enough of sieges with defective artillery and will never undertake another without the best. Therefore, in all my letters I have desired either 29 pounders, 9 feet long, Carron manufacture or 29 pounders, 8 feet long of the same manufacture and Carron shot.'

Other iron works were set up, for example at Wilsontown in Lanarkshire and Muirkirk in Ayrshire. James Watt's steam engine was used to blow a blast of air into the furnace, giving it its name, the 'blast-furnace'. Two other discoveries helped the iron industry to develop. David Mushet, who experimented with new ways of producing iron, found black-band ironstone in large quantities in the parish of Old Monkland. It was rich in both coal and iron. Then James Neilson invented the hot-blast to drive heated air, instead of cold air, into the furnace. This created an even more intense heat. The coal in the mixture helped in the smelting and three times as much iron was produced with the same amount of fuel. Ironmasters invaded Old and New Monkland; their new furnaces were soon in operation, and Coatbridge, Airdrie and Motherwell appeared almost overnight.

Steel

In the 1880s, firms like Colville of Motherwell and Beardmore of Parkhead Forge began to produce steel cheaply. Steel is harder and tougher than iron, and began to be preferred for building the ships and bridges and engines of all kinds, for which central Scotland became famous.

Later all the iron and steel had to be made from imported ore, most of it from Sweden, and the iron and steel industries had to modernise and make new products. The Carron Iron Works no longer produced carronades, but turned instead to making the street pillar-box, and the bath and the stove for people's houses. Motherwell became the centre of the steel industry where one blast-furnace at Ravenscraig could produce a thousand tonnes a day. Its strip mill supplied sheet steel for other industries nearby, but in 1992 Ravenscraig closed and steel-making in Scotland virtually came to an end.

Coal

In the new industrial age 'coal became king'. Previously the country's wealth in coal had not been recognised and little had been mined. Suddenly, ironmasters were calling out for more coal to feed their furnaces and foundries. Manufacturers needed it for the steam engines which drove the machinery in their factories. Railway engines devoured it. Gas-lighting in streets and homes was produced from it. More and more people wanted coal to burn in their grates, especially when transport by canals and railways made it cheaper over a wider area.

James Watt's steam engine, which itself ran on coal, proved of immense value to the mining industry:

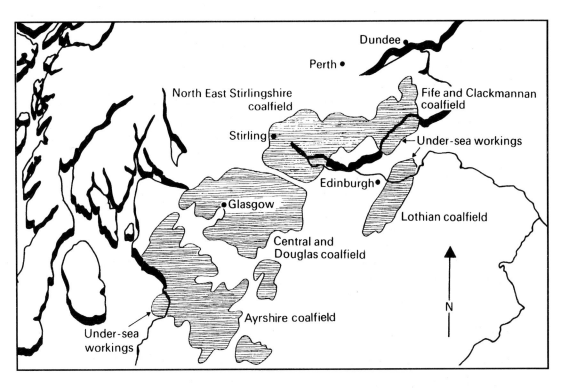

Coalfields of Central Scotland

1. for pumping water out of mines, and so allowing coal to be cut from seams deeper down in the ground,
2. for lifting coal from the depths to the surface.

The map above shows where the coalfields are. That is also where most of the towns are and where most people live. Many industries were established on coalfields because they needed coal as fuel or else made use of its by-products, and for over 150 years most Scottish industries depended on coal.

The coal mines were nationalised with high hopes in 1947, to be run by the National Coal Board on behalf of the people and in 1955 Scottish miners were producing 22 million tonnes of coal a year. Since about 1958, however, the demand for coal has declined as diesel and electric trains, oil heating, and electricity using gas, nuclear and hydro power have come into use more and more. By 1990 coal output in Scotland had fallen to 7.1 million tonnes, the one deep coal mine still working providing fuel for Longannet electricity station.

35

The Industrial Revolution: Transport

Cars, buses and lorries on the roads, and trains, aeroplanes and ships for longer journeys – all are in use every day to transport people and raw materials and manufactured goods to their destinations. These ways of moving goods and people are quite modern. They were created as a result of the Industrial Revolution.

As long as Scotland was an agricultural country the people in each village produced nearly everything they needed to support themselves, and they did not need to have much to do with the next village or town. The sea and the rivers were the oldest means of trading and travelling. Ships kept close to the coast and could come inland by sailing up the bigger rivers. When the Clyde was made deeper, for example, ships were able to reach the heart of Glasgow. But places farther away from the sea or a river had to be joined by canals, roads or railways to help trade between them.

Canals

In 1790 the 'navvies', as the men who cut canals or inland navigations were called, had been digging for years, and the Forth and Clyde Canal was ready. The Canal made it possible for ships to pass from the North Sea to the Atlantic between Grangemouth on the Forth and Bowling on the Clyde. The Union Canal from Edinburgh joined it at Falkirk in 1822 and connected Edinburgh and Glasgow by inland waterway. This was a good new way of carrying goods such as coal, iron and manufactured articles from the industrial towns and bringing in grain, flour and building materials, like granite and slate. People

Tall ships passing up Neptune's Staircase, the flight of eight locks on the Caledonian Canal

enjoyed travelling by canal. The passenger-boats were quicker and more comfortable than stage-coaches on the roads between Glasgow and Edinburgh.

The Monkland Canal connected Glasgow with the rich coal and iron deposits around Coatbridge and Airdrie, and made coal cheaper in the city. Two other canals are in the Highlands. The Caledonian along the Great Glen was the work of William Jessop and Thomas Telford, and the Crinan across Argyll was built by John Rennie and completed by Telford. Neither was as profitable as the canals in the Lowlands, which prospered until the railways came. Only the Highland canals remain open and they are busy with pleasure craft now but plans are afoot for the Millennium Link, the project to restore the Forth and Clyde–Union Canal waterway across central Scotland.

Roads

Until the eighteenth century practically no new roads had been built in Scotland since Roman times. Tracks simply became roads: roads were not made. People transported goods on their backs or in wicker baskets on the backs of pack-horses, or else on sledges. Before 1750 the appearance of a cart or carriage with spoked wheels was so unusual that people stopped work to watch one go past. Travel by road was very slow. In 1749 the journey between Edinburgh and Glasgow took 12 hours, whereas an express bus's time today is one hour ten minutes.

In the south of Scotland roads were improved by Turnpike Trusts. A turnpike was a wooden bar stretching across the road to stop horses and carts entering until payment had been made. Every traveller had to pay a toll to the keeper, and the money was used to repair and improve the roads. Tollhouses and old milestones on the roadsides, and a place-name like Tollcross, all remind us of the days of the Turnpike Trusts, which in 1858 maintained over 9,500 kilometres of roads.

More military roads were built in the Highlands after the 'Forty-five rising. They opened up the Highlands, not to encourage industry and trade but to keep the Highlanders at peace.

Two Scotsmen, Thomas Telford and John Loudon McAdam, did a great deal to improve transport and travel. Telford, a shepherd's son from Westerkirk near Langholm, trained to be a stone-mason. After working at his trade for a time on Edinburgh's New Town and Somerset House in London, he turned to building canals. He became an engineer with William Jessop on the Ellesmere Canal in Shropshire and later gave advice on the Göta Canal in Sweden.

In the Highlands he built many fine harbours, roads and bridges in order to encourage trade. As a result, ploughs and carts were introduced where they had not been known before. Regular coaches, running between Inverness and Perth, for example, connected the Highlands with the south. Above all, he provided jobs for 3,000 men a year. They learned to use tools and make roads in what Telford was proud to call his 'working academy'.

He set his mind to consider the three main problems in making roads – gradient, drainage and materials.

The main obstacles to the road builder are rivers and hills. Rivers can be bridged, and Telford built many great bridges. A road may go over a hill, as Roman roads did, or else round it. Making roads for traffic drawn by horses, Telford preferred to go round the side of a hill to make the gradient as gentle as possible. The result was a winding road with sharp bends in places. These are dangerous for motor traffic, which Telford could not foresee.

Until Telford's time, roads became rivers of mud in wet weather: he countered this by using small stones to make a smooth surface. He also gave the road a slight slope downwards from the crown to let the surface water run off into a ditch at either side. This curve on the road is called the 'camber'.

Telford believed in laying a firm foundation of stone blocks, covered by a 15cm layer of broken stones with a carpet of small stones on top.

John Loudon McAdam, on the other hand, thought Telford's foundation of stone blocks was expensive and unnecessary. He built roads directly on the ground, putting down a layer, 15–30cm deep, of broken stones, each 'small enough to go into a navvy's mouth'.

The wheels of the traffic ground the stones down to make a smooth, solid, waterproof surface. Being simpler than Telford's roads, McAdam's were much cheaper and his method was adopted all over Britain. McAdam did not use tar, but his name is commemorated in the name of the material 'tarmacadam', which consists of small stones bound together by tar as they are crushed under the weight of a road-roller.

The roads Telford and McAdam built introduced the age of travel by stage-coach. Coaching inns along the new roads supplied meals for passengers and a change of horses. Coaches ran faster and faster until the time taken for the journey from Edinburgh to London was reduced from ten days to two and half. The coaching era did not last long, because horses could not last the pace set by the locomotive, the 'iron horse'.

Roads and Bridges Today

Modern roads have smooth surfaces of asphalt or concrete, both of which ensure quiet running for traffic. New roads are straighter to suit faster traffic, and motorways avoid passing through the centre of towns. Many fine old bridges have had to be widened or replaced. New suspension bridges such as the Forth Road Bridge and the Erskine Bridge have replaced ferries and carry heavy traffic quickly across great rivers. However, the increase in the number of vehicles crossing the Forth Bridge in a year to 19.5 million in 1995 (an increase of over 60 per cent since 1984), has led to a proposal for a new road bridge over the Forth.

Donkeys lightly loaded with sweeping brushes,
a comment on the state of the roads by James Howe

Railways

The railway was in use long before the invention of the railway engine, when it was found that a horse could pull more if the wagons ran on rails instead of along the road. Colleries often had short railways and after 1810 loads of coal were hauled a longer distance by horses from Kilmarnock to the coast at Troon.

George Stephenson, the inventor of *The Rocket* locomotive (an engine which was able to move) was the pioneer of railways in England. He chose a 'gauge' – that is, the distance between the two rails – of 4 ft. 8$\frac{1}{2}$in. (nearly 1$\frac{1}{2}$ metres), which is used throughout Britain today. He decided on it by measuring carts to find the commonest distance between their wheels. This was the same width as the wheel span of a Roman wagon used 1600 years earlier. The first railway for locomotives in Scotland was between Garnkirk and St Rollox Station in Glasgow, and George Stephenson came to drive the first engine, named after him for the event, when it was opened in 1831. Coal was carried to Glasgow more cheaply than by canal, and passengers also took to this new form of transport.

Glasgow and Edinburgh became railway centres from which new lines branched out, and the two cities were connected by rail in 1842. There was a craze for building railways, and many private railway companies were formed to build local lines. By 1850 the towns in the southern half of the country were linked by a network of railways. Stations often had to be built on the outskirts of towns; in some places in the country small stations appeared where no village existed before.

Traffic on canals was too slow to compete with trains. Railways proved of

Seven years in the making and opened in 1890, the Forth Bridge is a unique monument to engineering and construction skills

enormous value to trade, for example in the distribution of fish from Aberdeen. Travel by rail became popular, too. It gave people the chance to travel at great speed. This reached its peak in the Race to the North between two trains from London to Aberdeen in 1895. The train from Euston via Carlisle beat its East Coast rival by eight minutes, having travelled 865 kilometres in eight hours 32 minutes, at an average speed of 101km an hour!

With the coming of the Railway Age, villages and towns were brought closer, and people in the country no longer felt isolated. Trips to visit friends, or to the seaside or the country, or to use the growing number of shops in the towns changed the lives of the people and made Scotland seem a much smaller place.

Ships

'Aye, a grand ship and Clyde built!' That statement could have described the *Queen Elizabeth* or hundreds of other ships. The shipbuilders on the Clyde gained a reputation for craftsmanship which was the envy of their rivals.

How did the Clyde become the hub of the shipbuilding world? Part of the answer lay in the deepening of the river, part in having supplies of iron and steel close at hand and part in the engineering industry which developed early to build the engines to drive steamships.

Henry Bell was not the first to use a steam engine in a ship, but from 1812 his

Comet with its steam engine, tall funnel and two sails, carried passengers between Helensburgh, Port Glasgow and the Broomielaw in Glasgow at a steady 8km (5 miles) per hour. This meant the Clyde was the first river in Europe to have a steamboat service.

From 1830 onwards steamers were being built with iron hulls, and about 50 years later steel ships came in. The Cunard Company had its first steamships built in Clyde yards in the 1840s. They carried passengers and mail to America and were the fastest on the North Atlantic route. A hundred years later Cunard's *Queen Mary* and *Queen Elizabeth* crossed almost three times faster. The steam turbine, invented by Charles Parsons, marked another great step forward in marine engineering. The Clyde pleasure steamer, *King Edward*, which was launched in 1901, was the first passenger ship in the world to be driven by turbines.

Early steamships, however, were challenged by the finest of sailing ships, the clippers. These slim-bodied ships had broad sails and were faster than steamships when the wind favoured them. Hall of Aberdeen built many clippers for the China tea trade. They used to race round the Cape of Good Hope to be first to reach London with the new season's crop. When the Suez Canal was opened in 1869 it shortened the journey to the East, but sailing ships had difficulty in passing through it and had to be towed. The *Cutty Sark*, built at Dumbarton, was the most famous of the clippers. It has been preserved at Greenwich on the Thames after a sailing life of 50 years, and reminds us of the grace and majesty of ships in the days of sail.

It was the iron-hulled steamer which made the Clyde a shipbuilding centre. Shipyards expanded and marine engineering developed. The day had come when the best ships were built on the Clyde and their engines at sea were cared for by a Scottish engineer. Many of the shipbuilding companies had family names which became world-famous, such as Scott of Greenock, Thomson (later John Brown and Company) of Clydebank and Stephen of Linthouse.

What shipbuilding did to change a town can be seen in Govan. Until the 1850s it was a village of cottages with thatched roofs, the homes of handloom weavers and workers in the silk mill and dyeworks. Govan was an independent community, and in 1864 it became a burgh which ran its own affairs. Then changes came quickly. The shipbuilders arrived; the place became noisy as the clang of the hammer on metal stifled the pleasant clack of the shuttle. Shipyards, engineering works, the railway and tenements took the place of the thatched cottage and the quiet street. Dry docks were built where the main street used to be. People came in because there was work to be had. The rise in population was sudden, even alarming. In 1864 there were 9,000 people; in 1905 there were 91,000. In 1912 the town lost its identity and became part of Glasgow. The story of Govan shows how an industrial town grew out of an earlier village and explains how a city like Glasgow swelled by absorbing nearby burghs.

Between the two World Wars, fewer new ships were ordered and thousands of men on Clydeside were thrown out of work. In the 1930s, however, the greatest

British passenger steamers, *Queen Mary* and *Queen Elizabeth*, were launched, each over 80,000 tonnes.

Since then shipbuilders in Britain have had to face fierce competition from other countries – especially Japan, Germany, Korea, Holland and Sweden – and have lost the large share of the market they once had. In the mid-1950s, one ship out of every four in the world was built in a British yard: by mid-1970, Britain's share had fallen to one ship out of every 25. Whereas 31 ships were completed in 1979, the number in 1989 was only 11, with the result that the total number of workers employed in building and repairing ships in Scotland kept falling until it was down to 13,500 in 1989. The decline has continued.

To some extent the fall in ship-building jobs was cushioned by the need for men with similar skills to build huge production platforms of steel to extract the oil from the North Sea. As the oil industry now seems to have reached its peak, however, the demand for new platforms is low.

Visits

Glasgow Transport Museum, in Bunhouse Road behind the Kelvin Hall, has an outstanding collection of locomotives and vehicles. The Royal Museum of Scotland in Chambers Street, Edinburgh, is good for models of locomotives and ships.

Queuing for unemployment insurance at Clydebank, 1932
(courtesy of West Dunbartonshire Libraries Department)

36

The French Revolution and Scotland

In France in the 1780s the king *was* the government. He ruled the country as he pleased, and his officials carried out his orders. The different social classes – clergy, nobles and peasants – were separate and unequal. The nobles, for example, escaped paying some taxes altogether but had no part to play in government. The peasants were poor, under a crushing burden of taxes, but they had no rights, because the States-General, as the French parliament was called, had not met for over 170 years.

True, many people were talking about better government. Educated men, such as lawyers, doctors, teachers, merchants and some noblemen, were struck by the ideas of thinkers like Rousseau who wrote *The Social Contract*. He thought the people should share in making the laws and the king in turn should be guided by them.

Events in France

But after a century of wars, France was nearly bankrupt, spending far more every year than was raised in taxes. What was to be done? The king, Louis XVI, well-meaning but weak-willed, was not the man for the task. When he asked the nobles to pay more taxes, they refused and he was forced at last to call a meeting of the States-General. Its members were asked to bring lists of the people's grievances and they brought thousands of them. France was ripe for reform but the king had no programme to offer them.

The pace quickened. On 14 July 1789, the crowds in Paris seized weapons and captured the Bastille, the great prison which seemed to them a symbol of tyranny. Castles and mansions all over the country were ransacked and set on fire, and many nobles fled from France. July 14 was declared a national holiday, and a new flag of blue, white and red – the Tricolour – came into use. Unfair taxes and the privileges of the nobles were swept away. Many peasants now became the owners of their farms. Following the example of the Americans, the members drew up a 'Declaration of the Rights of Man'; following the British, they were working out a system of government by king and parliament together.

Events in France held the attention of the world. The nation had experienced a complete change, a revolution. Tyranny and feudalism had been overthrown.

'All men are free,' the French people cried, 'all men are equal, all men are brothers.'

Their victory was not yet complete. The Revolution had enemies at home and abroad: it was soon to be baptised in blood. The royal family escaped in 1791 but were captured and forced to return. Austria, home of the French Queen, Marie Antoinette, threatened to intervene. The French accepted the challenge and declared 'war against tyrants, peace with all peoples'. France became a republic in 1792 and then the king was put to death. The new republic tried to strengthen itself by turning against everyone who had supported the king. No one was safe. In the Reign of Terror (1792–94) thousands met their deaths by the guillotine.

At first the war went badly for France, as one country after another, including Britain, joined the alliance against her. The Revolution was in danger but France stood firm. Her great new armies, well-trained and well-equipped, fought with burning zeal for liberty and the glory of France. Soon they were to conquer under the military genius of Napoleon.

Storming the Bastille, 14 July 1789 (The Mansell Collection/Time Inc./Katz)

*Thomas Muir
(detail from a
drawing by David
Martin. Courtesy of
the Scottish National
Portrait Gallery)*

What Scotland Thought

At first, news of the events in France was received with pleasure in Britain. The French appeared to be following Britain's example in demanding to be ruled with the advice of parliament, as Britain had been since 'The Glorious, Bloodless Revolution' a century before.

Within a fortnight of the capture of the Bastille, Glasgow newspapers were already using the word 'revolution' to describe what was happening in France. Looking back on it later, Lord Cockburn, a Whig lawyer, summed up how large it loomed in people's minds, when he wrote:

> Everything rang, and was connected with the Revolution in France; which, for above 20 years, was, or was made, the all in all. Everything, literally everything was soaked in this one event.

In his book *The Rights of Man*, an Englishman, Tom Paine, defended the French Revolution. This work proved very popular in Scotland, as Alexander Wilson, the Paisley weaver-poet, tells us:

> The Rights of Man is now well kenned
> And read by mony a hunder
> For Tammy Paine the buik has penned
> And lent the court a lounder [hard knock].

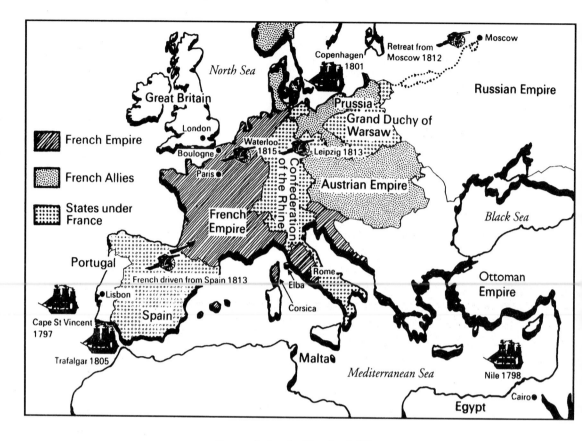

Europe during the Napoleonic Wars

Robert Burns was delighted by the rising of the French people. He even sent guns – four carronades – for the French to use in their struggle, but they were seized by Customs officials at Dover. In several of his poems he shares the ideals of the French, especially where he declares:

> For a' that, and a' that,
> It's comin' yet for a' that
> That man to man, the world o'er
> Shall brothers be for a' that!

Thinking about freedom and equality, many men in Britain became dissatisfied with the government as it was. They were not revolutionaries but reformers. They did not want to overthrow the government but they did want to reform Parliament to make it represent more people. They founded the 'Society of the Friends of the People'. In England, its members were well-off and could afford to pay a subscription of two guineas (£2.10) a year. In Scotland it cost much less, only a shilling (5p), and:

Old toothless schoolmasters and furious tanners,
Tailors, hairdressers, deep-read butchers too,
All list [enlist] with zeal under fair Reform's banners
And that they will be great men vow.

The Society had far more working-class support in Scotland than in England. The government did nothing about the people's grievances, the wretched living and working conditions which accompanied the new industrial age. The Society called for a Parliament, in which they were represented, to put an end to their troubles. The government panicked and determined to capture the leaders. Of Thomas Muir, the lawyer who was the guiding hand of the Friends of the People in Scotland, the government's chief law officer wrote, 'I am resolved to lay him by the heels on a charge of High Treason'. Muir was arrested and sentenced by Lord Braxfield to 14 years' transportation. His crime was not treason: he was merely proposing that Parliament should be chosen by the people as it is today. People were outraged at such severe punishment, and Fox, the Whig leader, exclaimed, 'God help the people who have such judges!'

The story of Muir's life is so dramatic that it would make an exciting film. It included his voyage on a convict ship to Botany Bay in Australia, his rescue by an American ship, and a sea-fight off the coast of Spain when he lost the sight of an eye. At last he arrived in France to throw in his lot with the revolutionaries.

At home, people's ideas changed. The Reign of Terror disgusted many people who had previously been in sympathy with the Revolution. When the war brought the risk of the French invading, Robert Burns was one of those who enlisted in the volunteers to defend the land, and he wrote a patriotic song:

Does haughty Gaul invasion threat
Then let the louns beware, sir
There's wooden walls upon our seas
And volunteers on shore, sir . . .

Who will not sing, *God save the King*
Shall hang as high's the steeple
But while we sing *God save the King*
We'll ne'er forget the people!

Reform in the people's cause, however, was out of the question until the war was won, and that was not until 1815 when Napoleon's armies were finally defeated at the Battle of Waterloo. Nevertheless, the British learned from the French that the people have certain rights. To achieve them the French had taken up arms and overthrown their government, but in Britain, as we will see, no revolution took place.

37

The Rise of Glasgow

The Bishop's Burgh

The rise of Glasgow has been recent and rapid. At the time of the Union its inhabitants numbered 13,000, about the same as Prestwick, Fraserburgh or Galashiels today. It was a pleasant town lying between the Cathedral and the Clyde. In the Middle Ages it was the bishop's burgh, looking up to the high spire of the Cathedral on the ridge. Below the Cathedral were the manses of clergy such

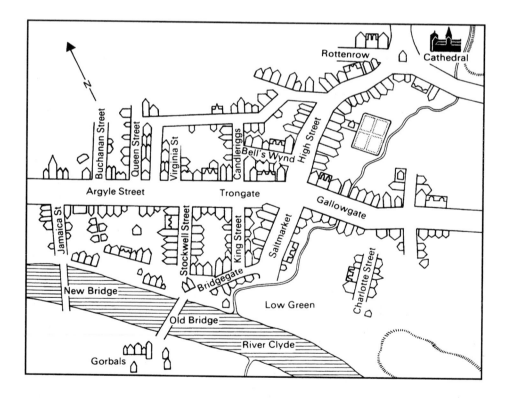

Glasgow in the 1780s

as the Parson of Stobo, whom we met earlier (*see* pages 116–17). Of these houses only Provand's Lordship remains. Down the High Street four roads met at Glasgow Cross. The High Street, which continued towards the river as the Saltmarket, was crossed from the west by the Trongate, and from the east by the Gallowgate which was named from the site of the town gallows. Glasgow had a weekly market, and merchants thronged to its great Fair starting on 7 July, the date of the dedication of the Cathedral. As the population increased tenements were built in the region of the Cross, but the town was not crowded.

The Trading Town

Daniel Defoe was impressed by Glasgow. In *A Tour through that Part of Great Britain called Scotland* (1727), he called it:

> one of the cleanest, most beautiful and best-built cities in Great Britain . . . The four principal streets are the fairest for breadth and the finest built that I have ever seen in one city together. The houses are all of stone . . . The lower storeys for the most part stand on vast Doric columns with the arches which open into the shops, adding to the strength as well as beauty of the building.

The pillars and arches Defoe admired were like those in Gladstone's Land in Edinburgh (*see* page 170). This was a time when some Scottish industries were not doing well. Scottish woollens, for example, could not compete with finer English cloth. Fife had lost its 'golden fringe' because its fishing ports had few salt herrings to sell abroad. At this time, too, the burgh of Culross, described in chapter 27, fell asleep. But Glasgow flourished. Not yet a port itself, it created one 32km nearer the sea at Newark Bay, which became Port Glasgow in 1668. Glasgow looked west across the Atlantic to the English colonies in America, and there its future lay.

The colonies in America and the West Indies were previously allowed to trade only with England. In 1707 they were opened to the Scots as well. Glasgow merchants were quick to seize this opportunity. They bought ships to bring in tobacco from Virginia and sugar from the West Indies. Little of the tobacco was sold in this country, most being re-exported to France and other countries in Europe, which were not allowed to trade directly with British colonies at that time.

Tobacco merchants became wealthy. Decked in red cloaks, cocked hats and powdered wigs, these 'tobacco lords', as they were called, were recognised as a class apart, men who were making fortunes. They built fine houses west of the old town and some bought country estates.

They were not the only people who profited from this trade. It brought wealth into the country, which encouraged new industries, especially in Glasgow. The colonists needed goods which they could not produce for themselves, and Glasgow started making leather, glass bottles, tape, nails and pottery. Nearby,

Anderston and Paisley produced linen. Glasgow exported nearly two million metres of linen a year to the colonies where the plantation slaves worked in coarse linen shirts.

In 1775 the tobacco trade ended with a crash. The American colonists at Concord fired the first shots in their struggle for freedom from Britain. Many of the 'tobacco lords' were ruined, but they had done their work. They had 'primed the pump' by providing the money which had started new industries in the town.

The American War did not mark the end of the road for Glasgow. Men were at work building jetties to narrow the channel of the Clyde and make it deeper. Combined with intensive dredging, this deepened the river to 4.2m. In this way Glasgow 'made the Clyde' and became its own port.

The Industrial Town

After tobacco, businessmen turned to manufacturing cotton and Glasgow and district became the Lancashire of Scotland. By 1830 many new mills were built in the city. They were driven by steam engines instead of water-power and the smoke from their tall chimneys spread over the town.

The steam engine also helped Glasgow to become her own port. By 1830, 25 steamships were operating on the Clyde and scores of steam tugs shepherded sailing ships up and down the narrow channel of the river.

At the same time the iron industry was developing in Lanarkshire. By using the hot-blast furnace, seven times as much iron was being produced in 1845 as in 1835. Here was the material for building iron ships and their engines, and railway locomotives as well. This was the beginning of the great period when Clydeside built for the world.

Housing the People

In modern times, when a town is bigger than its neighbours it tends to become bigger still. Glasgow was already a port and soon it was supplied with roads, canals and railways. Telford's new road to Carlisle allowed stage-coaches to run direct to London; the Monkland Canal linked Glasgow with the coal and iron around Coatbridge and Airdrie, and by 1842 it had become a railway centre as well. People came in from the countryside; others, displaced by sheep in the Highlands, arrived; as well as a great many driven out by poverty in Ireland. Glasgow attracted them all like a magnet. The town grew in size and the population became more mixed as Highlanders, Irish labourers, Jews and immigrants from Central Europe came to settle.

The easiest way to house them was to divide up existing houses to take in more families and lodgers. From 1840 onwards solid tenements, new blocks of homes, were being built farther out but the centre of the city was far too crowded. A

Thatched cottages near the Cathedral in the early 1800s (by courtesy of the Mitchell Library, Glasgow City Libraries and Archives)

visitor to a house up a dark close there found it so small that he could not believe it and he asked if he could measure it:

> We put the right heel against the toe of the left shoe, and found that six shoe-lengths determine the breadth, and between eight and nine the length from the bed to the fireplace. The height of the room scarcely allows us to stand upright. In this hole the husband and wife have lived for one or two years, and two children.

Overcrowding made it easier for disease to spread and caused more infants to die than in most other big cities in Europe. Typhus fever broke out periodically among the poor in dirty, crowded homes. Three times between 1832 and 1854 cholera, which is caused by polluted water, claimed thousands of lives. The Town Council declared war on dirt. It brought in a clean water supply in pipes all the way from Loch Katrine and built a great sewerage scheme to pipe waste away underground. In 1863 the first Medical Officer of Health was appointed. Gradually these changes and the demolition of the worst slum property made the city cleaner and the people healthier.

Many of the tenements, however, were lived in far longer than they should have been. Here is a description by William Bolitho of a 'single-end', a one-roomed house, in one of them in 1924:

A small room, one end of which is taken up by the Scots' fireplace, like an enclosed iron altar, with two hobs on which the teapot is kept everlastingly on the boil. The floor is worn wood, there are irregular square inches of frayed oilcloth. An enormous drabbled woman, who is dressed in dish clothes which do not show the dirt so plainly, however, as her face, explains the arrangements . . . She has five children, and the gas is kept burning all day at the glimmer. The elements are simple and human. There is the bed, set into a niche, deep, evil-smelling, strewed with heaps of the same material as her dress . . . Bed, hearth, and chair: humanity's minimum, as simple as the Parables. Under the window is the 'jaw box', the boarded, greasy sink, with polished syphon tap . . . On the mantelpiece are two china dogs.

Glasgow before 1914

Before 1914 the city held an important position in the world of trade and industry. A great exhibition in 1901 put Glasgow's achievements on show in Kelvingrove Museum and Art Gallery, which was built specially. Other great buildings had gone up like the City Chambers and the Mitchell Library. The Glasgow School of Art, which was opened in 1907, was one of the first buildings in Europe in a truly modern style. It was designed by Charles Rennie Mackintosh, a Glasgow architect whose fame became international.

A single-end, formerly on display in Old Glasgow Museum
(by courtesy of the People's Palace Museum)

The Corporation tramways – 'the caurs' – were electrified and became a model for other cities. For holidays on the Clyde coast, trains and steamers provided frequent services at remarkable speeds. In the suburbs more roomy tenements were being erected, and before 1914 Glasgow had its own garden suburb at Westerton.

As time passed more industries and people crowded into Glasgow. The city needed more space. It spread, sprawling over the countryside until former villages and towns found themselves inside its boundaries. Villages such as Port Dundas and towns such as Anderston, Hillhead, Maryhill, Pollokshaws and Govan became parts of the great city, and the open land between them provided building sites for factories and foundries, and – after the First World War – for council houses and bungalows as well. The area was almost all built up, and Glasgow's population became too big for the city to hold.

Glasgow had grown very quickly into a lively, bustling city. After the Irish Potato Famine in 1845 particularly, great numbers of Irish families came to stay and were willing to take any job they could get. Most of them were Catholic and the number of Catholics in the city, thought to be about 40,000 in 1840, rose rapidly and seven new chapels were built for them in the next 20 years. The number of Protestant churches increased also, and not only to meet the needs of incomers to the city.

In 1843 the Church of Scotland split, when 470 ministers led by Dr Thomas Chalmers, former minister of St John's in Glasgow, broke away. They set up the Free Church of Scotland and soon there were several new Free Church congregations in Glasgow. Orangemen's Lodges flourished among Protestant skilled workers who usually succeeded in keeping apprenticeships for their own sons.

Drink, then football, became the people's passion. In Glasgow in 1843 there was one public house for every 130 people and the common drink was whisky. The churches and the temperance movement fought against it but it was the heavy tax on whisky in 1909 which started the decline in whisky-drinking. In football, Queen's Park F.C. was founded in 1867, Partick Thistle in 1868, Rangers in 1872 and Celtic in 1887, and when Celtic built its stadium in the 1890s it had space for 70,000 people to come and watch the team play.

Glasgow since 1945

In 1951 the city contained well over one million of Scotland's total population of just over five million. Every fifth Scot 'belonged to Glasgow'. Glasgow is still the industrial capital of Scotland. Half of her industry is concentrated inside a radius of about 30 kilometres from the city.

By the standards of the 1950s, Glasgow was overcrowded. It did not have room to build enough good houses for all its people, even when some of the new houses were in high rise-blocks, as in the Gorbals. The solution proposed was for 70,000 families to 'overspill' from Glasgow to new towns not far away, such as East

Kilbride or Cumbernauld, or to smaller towns farther away, such as Wick and Haddington. It was important to provide jobs as well as houses for the people who agreed to leave Glasgow. Most people who moved to a new life elsewhere seemed to be happy to have done so. So many had moved out that by 1991 the population of Glasgow had fallen to below 700,000. Many industries in the city have closed, great areas of tenements have been knocked down and the city is rebuilding and renewing itself inside its own boundaries.

Visits

To see the story of Glasgow in its buildings, go first to the Cathedral (*see* the map on page 198), parts of which are 700 years old. Next, take a look at the Tolbooth Steeple, down the High Street at Glasgow Cross, all that remains of the old meeting-place of the Town Council 300 years ago. In these buildings of grey stone quarried in the district you see the old centre of Glasgow, the Glasgow of the bishop, the minister and the 'tobacco lord'. Round it arose this great Victorian City with its impressive City Chambers and University, its churches, and its bold commercial and industrial buildings, which are well worth exploring. Lastly, go and see the Burrell Collection in Pollok Country Park (buses run from Union Street), the greatest treasure of objects and pictures ever given to a city by one man.

European City of Culture in 1990, Glasgow is the home of the Royal Scottish National Orchestra, Scottish Opera and Scottish Ballet.

Kelvingrove Art Gallery and Museum, opened in 1901 (by courtesy of the Mitchell Library, Glasgow City Libraries and Archives)

38

Agriculture, Industry and the People

How did the new ways of farming and making things affect people's lives? A modern poet, William Montgomerie, has written that it was a time:

> when field and glen
> Squeezed out their starving surplus [extra people], and for food
> The mill took payment from the souls of men;
> When Scottish children lived the stunted [shortened or deprived] years
> Between a factory and a city slum;
> When earth by smoke was curtained off from heaven.

Country Labourers

Few working people have written about their lives but in his book, *The Autobiography of a Working Man*, Alexander Somerville recalls his early years in East Lothian. He remembers the one-roomed house where his parents and their eight children lived, ate and slept. It had no ceiling and no floor except for the bare earth. The only window and the fire-bars, which went across the front of the fire, belonged to his father and he took them with him when they moved from one house to another. To pay the rent his mother had to cut corn during the harvest and carry sheaves to the barn for a whole month when the grain was being threshed.

Alexander's father was earning 15 shillings (75p) a week as a mason's labourer in 1810, but food was so dear that he could not afford the shilling (5p) fee to register the boy's birth. When Alexander was five the potato crop was poor, and all the family had for dinner each day was bad potatoes and one or two salt herrings cut up between them. He did not go to school until he was seven, because he had no decent clothes to wear, and he left the next summer to herd cows. In winter he returned to school, but in his early years he had far more of farm-work than book-learning. Soon he was doing a man's work: he harrowed and ploughed, he dug drains for seven shillings (35p) a week, he mowed hay and cut corn all the hours of daylight, sleeping in barns and walking from farm to farm in East Lothian and Berwickshire. Weary from his labours and not having enough to eat, he looked for a way of escape. He found one by 'taking the King's shilling' and enlisting in the Scots Greys in 1831.

Girls carrying coal underground (courtesy of the Trustees of the National Library of Scotland)

Workers in Coal Mines

Walter Pryde was 81, a great age for a coal-miner to reach in 1842. Many miners were dead by the age of 40. He remembered that he was nine years old when he started work at Preston Grange Colliery in East Lothian. 'We were then all slaves to the Preston Grange laird,' he said. People like him could not go away anywhere else to work but had to work where and when the laird told them. He recalled that men who disobeyed 'were placed by the necks in iron collars, called "juggs", and fastened to the wall'. Not until 1799 did the miners gain their freedom.

Even then, their children still worked underground and did not feel free. One of them, 11-year-old Janet Cumming, said she had 'no liking for the work; father makes me like it'. Janet worked from five in the morning to five at night and all night on Fridays. She carried the coal on her back in a basket called a creel from where her father cut it to the place where it would be taken up to the surface.

> The weight is usually a hundredweight; I do not know now many pounds there are in a hundredweight, but it is some weight to carry. The distance varies, sometimes 150 fathoms [about 275 metres]; whiles 250 fathoms. The roof is very low; I have to bend my back and legs . . .

Agnes Moffat was 17. She had worked underground since she was ten. Her job was to carry coal in a basket on her back up one ladder after another. 'Sometimes,' she said, 'women lose their load and drop off the ladder. Margaret McNeil did a few weeks ago and injured both her legs. The lasses hate the work but they canna run away from it.'

These children went home tired. Not that home was much to look forward to. A single room with little furniture, no water in the house, no decent sanitation, steaming clothes drying by the fire, dirt everywhere – that was home, just like the next house and the next and the next in a cheaply built 'miners' row'.

Children in Factories

David Dale's spinning factory at New Lanark was better than most in the 1790s, for he was a more caring employer. The factory was clean and airy. Of the children who worked for him, most lived in the village with their parents, but about 400, who were orphans from the cities, lived in a boarding-house. They slept three in a bed. They were well fed and well clothed, although like most other children they went barefoot in summer.

The children worked for eleven and a half hours a day, from six in the morning until seven at night with an hour and a half for meals. Each evening after supper they went to school until nine o'clock, to learn to read, write and count; and on Sundays they spent three hours on Bible lessons. Children who lived with their parents received a wage, but the orphans worked in return for their keep and education. When they became 15 they were free to go off to other jobs if they wished. Many of the boys stayed on in the textile industry to become apprentice weavers.

Their conditions probably shock you. They shocked Robert Owen. This clever Welshman came to New Lanark after learning all about the new cotton-spinning machines in Lancashire. He married David Dale's daughter and in 1799 he bought New Lanark Mills.

He found that few of the children learned anything in school so late at night,

Dancing in Owen's school (courtesy of New Lanark Conservation Trust)

and that many fell asleep because they were so tired. He did not allow any children to work in the factory until they were ten years old. Instead they went to school during the day to learn to read and write and count, and to sing and dance as well. He believed that the more they learned, and enjoyed learning, the better workers they would become. With teachers interested in their welfare they also grew into better people. The children were happy in school and they thought the world of Robert Owen. When they were old enough to work, their hours in the factory were not too long to prevent them from profiting from evening classes in school after work.

The New Town-Dwellers

As we can imagine, the people who were squeezed out from the country into the new towns found their conditions of life hard to bear. The working day was long. Wages might not be as low as in the country but the plentiful number of workers coming in to compete for jobs helped to keep wages in central Scotland lower than in comparable parts of England. That was true in 1850, and it was still true in 1886 for building workers and shipyard workers alike. Their homes were often overcrowded and insanitary. Out of every three families in Glasgow in 1914, one was still living in a one-roomed house and one in a two-roomed house, and families were large in those days.

Often the worker's house belonged to his employer. If he lost his job he was forced to leave his home as well. He had many fears – the fear of the rent-collector, the fear of disease, and the fear of unemployment due to a slump in trade or to the arrival of more Irish immigrants who would work for lower wages. The weak-hearted turned to cheap whisky to drown their fears, but the serious 'well-doing' tradesman considered his situation more carefully, and was prepared to support any movement which might improve his way of life.

Visits

It is still possible to visit nineteenth-century workers' houses in different parts of Scotland. Hugh Millar's at Cromarty, north of Inverness, for example, was the home of a stonemason; in Shuttle Street, Kilbarchan, near Glasgow, is a weaver's cottage; and at Kirkoswald in Ayrshire a shoemaker's, on whom Robert Burns based the character Souter Johnnie in *Tam o' Shanter*. In Glasgow at 145 Buccleuch Street, Garnethill, is a good quality tenement house, built a hundred years ago.

Among workplaces which can be visited is the Lady Victoria coalmine at Newtongrange on the A7 near Edinburgh.

39

The Struggle for Reform: What People Did for Themselves

If all employers had been like Robert Owen, or even David Dale, working conditions could have improved rapidly, but Owen was thought to be a 'crank' and few employers followed his example. To make a profit, they felt they needed to have complete control over their workers, the right to 'hire them and fire them' and to decide how long they should work and how much they should be paid.

Trade Unions

A worker on his own was weak compared with his employer. Workers realised that if they banded together with others in the same trade or industry they might force their employers to pay higher wages or make the working day shorter. Therefore they formed trade unions.

Members of an early trade union, the Association of Cotton Spinners of Glasgow and Neighbourhood, went on strike in 1837. Their aim was to prevent the introduction of bigger machines which they feared would lead to lower wages and unemployment. Some tried to set fire to factories and fought other workmen brought in to take their places. When the leaders were arrested, the sentence of transportation for seven years for trying to persuade people to strike, frightened others out of trade union activity. Instead they began to work for the reform of parliament or the improvement of people's working conditions by acts passed by parliament.

Alexander MacDonald, who started work in a coal-mine at the age of eight, became a great leader of the miners. In 1863 he united all the miners of Great Britain in the National Union of Mineworkers. When he became a Member of Parliament he fought to win rights for trade unions to bargain with employers on behalf of their members and to go on strike without their leaders running the risk of being imprisoned. These rights were won in 1875.

Many improvements, especially in wages and hours of work, have been due to collective bargaining between trade unions and employers. If agreement can be achieved without a strike, it is less harmful to product output and to the pockets of the workers.

VOTE FOR

Home Rule.

Democratic
Government.

Justice to Labour

No Monopoly.

No Landlordism

Temperance
Reform.

Healthy Homes.

Fair Rents.

Eight-Hour Day.

Work for the
Unemployed.

KEIR HARDIE

What Keir Hardie stood for at West Ham in 1892 (by kind permission of the National Museum of Labour History)

Trade unions also helped working men to become Members of Parliament (before MPs were paid). Their hope was that Parliament would pass Acts which would help the working classes. One of the first Labour MPs was Keir Hardie. As a young Scottish miner who read widely, he learned to think for himself and to argue sensibly. Often he was chosen by his fellow-miners to speak for them to their employer, who regarded him as the workers' leader and a trouble-maker. He and his brothers were dismissed. When no mine-owner in the district would employ him, he became the organiser of the miners. He soon realised that the voice of the worker must be heard in Parliament, and in 1888 he founded the Scottish Labour Party, the first in Britain. But he failed to persuade enough Scottish voters to vote for him and he had to go to England to win a seat. He became MP for West Ham in 1892 and the cloth cap he wore when he turned up among the top-hatted Members of the House of Commons announced that the age of the working man had dawned. He forged the link between the trade unions and the Labour Party, and today the unions support the Labour Party in Parliament.

Friendly Societies

Some unions, such as the one formed by the stonemasons, used their funds to give help to their members, and men who were out of work were paid six shillings (30p) a week. Other men joined groups called Friendly Societies to help one another in time of need. If a man paid his subscription regularly he qualified for sick pay when he was ill and a pension when he was too old to work. Some societies encouraged their members to save. On one day a year – 'the cauvin' o' the coo', as it was called – they divided up their funds and so helped members to pay their rents. Several friendly societies, like the Oddfellows and the Free Gardeners, still exist.

The Co-operative Societies

As early as 1812 some people at Lennoxtown in Stirlingshire formed a Victualling Society which bought food in bulk to sell directly to those who joined them. This cut out the profit the wholesaler or middleman usually made. Prices could be lower and people got more for their money. Each member also received a share of the profits. The amount, called the 'dividend', depended on how much he or she had spent. This idea of co-operative trading became popular and co-operative stores were set up in many towns.

Then in 1868 the Scottish Co-operative Wholesale Society was founded to supply goods as cheaply as possible to the local societies. Soon it began to manufacture some goods as well, such as shoes, furniture, biscuits and clothes. In 1973 it became part of the British society, the Co-operative Wholesale Society, which owns tea and cocoa plantations as well as factories and creameries. Today supermarket chains also buy in bulk and distribute in bulk all over the country and the Co-op finds it more difficult to compete with them.

By forming trade unions and friendly societies and supporting the Co-operative movement, thousands of workmen were doing their best to help themselves before the government recognised that it had a duty to help them.

Visit

The People's Palace Museum on Glasgow Green, a treasure house on people's lives at home and at work, is also fascinating for evidence on movements for change in this and the following two chapters.

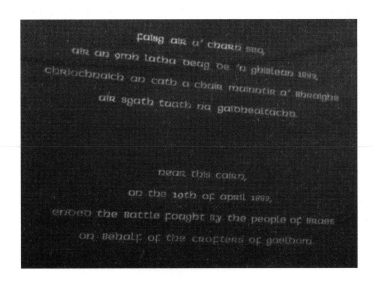

Memorial to the Battle of the Braes (1882) in Skye – after it, crofters became secure on their crofts at fair rents by 1886

40

The Struggle for Reform of Parliament and Councils

Parliament

If workers looked to Parliament to improve their lot before 1830, they looked in vain. Parliament did not represent the people and never had done.

As more people moved into industrial towns, Parliament became more unrepresentative than ever. The workers had no votes: the new towns had no MPs. By 1831, Glasgow had a population of over 200,000 but still shared one MP with three little burghs nearby – Renfrew, Rutherglen and Dumbarton. The only town to have a Member of its own was Edinburgh and he was chosen by the Town Council. No one else had any share in the election. In the counties of Scotland, only landowners had the right to vote. Out of the two and a quarter million people in Scotland in 1830 only about 4,000 landowners and town councillors took part in choosing Scotland's 45 MPs. That meant that each MP represented fewer than a hundred voters: today, he or she represents about 50,000.

Especially in the industrial towns, Scotsmen wanted the right to vote. Just as they had been active during the French Revolution, they rallied to the cause of Parliamentary reform. The Grand Procession in Glasgow to commemorate the Coronation of King William IV in 1831 was turned into a huge demonstration in favour of reform. A hundred thousand people were there on Glasgow Green. Five hundred carters led on horseback, followed by men of 50 different trades of the city, from chimney-sweeps to engineers, marching to the sound of music behind their trade banners. Some carried two different messages, the Felt Hatters for example, 'for the King and the Rights of the People', while the Potters claimed that people, like their pots, would become stronger through reform:

> We make our pots of what we Potters are,
> And strengthen clay, to stand the rudest storm,
> Passed through the needful furnace of Reform.

The whole procession was disciplined and orderly but the leaders of the movement for reform in London became worried and one of them, Francis Jeffrey, wrote to another, Lord Cockburn, 'For God's sake, keep the people quiet in Scotland'.

In 1832 the first Reform Act was passed and landowners and town councillors lost their right to elect all the MPs by themselves. Over the next century the right to vote was gradually extended to more and more men. Women first gained the right to vote in 1918 and ten years later all women over 21 gained equal voting rights with men. That was the position until the qualifying age for everyone was lowered to 18 in 1969.

Voting took place in public until the Ballot Act in 1872 gave people the right to vote in secret and without fear. Working men could not afford to try to become MPs at first, but since 1911 MPs have been paid.

REGISTER OF ELECTORS IN FORCE 16 FEB 1998 TO 15 FEB 1999

Parliamentary constituency   Edinburgh East
Regional division   Jock's Lodge/Portobello
Edinburgh district ward   Portobello

S before an Elector's name = Service Voter
M before an Elector's name = Merchant Seaman
The date when a young person reaches voting age appears immediately before the name. The Elector can vote at any election after that date.

VOTER'S NUMBER	STREET AND ELECTOR'S NAME **Brunstane Street**	STREET NUMBER
1066	McNab, Catherine	1
1067	McNab, John	1
1068	M– McNab, Robert J.	1
1069	Smith, Anne E.	2
1070	Smith, Kenneth J.	2
1071	15/1/99 Smith, Mary	2
1072	Smith, William B.	2
1073	Fisher, Andrew	3
1074	Fisher, Ellen C.	3

What the Register of Electors is like

Local Councils

Local affairs were run by local councils but in the old royal burghs, the people had no share in electing the town councils. Members of the council themselves decided who would be on the next council. No wonder people said 'Yince a bailie, aye a bailie!' In running the town's affairs, the councillors had to answer to no one but themselves. The townspeople had no way of finding out how the town's money was being spent. Sometimes, as in Aberdeen in 1817 after a great deal had been spent on the harbour and street improvements, people suddenly heard that their council was bankrupt. They felt they should have the right to choose their council members – and also to remove them at the next election.

In the royal burghs in 1833 every householder who paid a rent of £10 or more gained the right to vote in town council elections. Suddenly local elections became exciting occasions. The poster war began and in the cities people turned out to vote in their thousands. All other burghs which had not been royal burghs were given town councils in 1900. Town councils, and county councils since 1889 for rural areas, dealt with local affairs until local government reform in 1975 swept them all away.

Far fewer councils were set up in their place: nine regional councils, 53 district councils and three island councils. Everyone over 18 has the right to vote in one of these elections but to stand for election as a councillor or a Member of Parliament, it is necessary to be over the age of 21.

Demonstrators marching for votes for women as well as men in Princes Street, Edinburgh, 1909 (by courtesy of the People's Palace Museum)

41

The Struggle for Reform: What Parliament Did

Child Labour

After the first Reform Act 1832, Parliament began to remove the worst evils of the industrial age. Children under the age of nine were not allowed to work in textile factories at all by the Factory Act of 1833, and those under 13 were not to work more than 48 hours a week. This did not satisfy reformers like Lord Shaftesbury. He was the son of a rich landowner and succeeded to his father's wealth and title. He was shocked by what working children had to endure and he devoted his whole energy to making their lives better.

Lord Shaftesbury's greatest achievement was the Mines Act of 1842. Boys had to be ten years old before they could be employed in a coal mine, and women and girls were stopped from working underground. He also prevented little boys going up chimneys to sweep them. Hours of work were reduced and standards of safety tightened up. Since Shaftesbury's time conditions in all industries have slowly become better. Not until 1901 did workers have a half day off work on Saturdays and it was only after the Second World War that Saturday became a day of leisure for most workers.

The Cost of Living

When Robert Peel became Prime Minister in 1841, he removed or reduced the customs duties on many goods imported from overseas. This reduced many prices, but to most workers the cost of bread was the main item in the cost of living. Since 1815 the hated Corn Laws had kept the price of bread high. Two Lancashire businessmen, Cobden and Bright, fought hard for foreign corn to come into Britain free of duty. In 1845 heavy rains spoiled the corn harvest, and in Ireland the potato crop rotted in the ground. Food was scarce and thousands starved. Next year Peel repealed the Corn Laws, and corn became cheaper.

Britain became 'the workshop of the world'. Being the first country to have an industrial revolution, she could produce goods for other nations more cheaply than they could for themselves.

This advantage encouraged her to extend her policy of free trade. She exported manufactured goods and benefited from cheap food and raw materials imported from the colonies and elsewhere.

Education

As the age at which children might start work was raised, Parliament began to do more to provide schools for them. True, there were many schools already, and Scotland was better off for schools than England. Most of the towns had burgh or grammar schools which were paid for partly by the town and partly from the pupils' fees but this was less common in the new industrial towns. In the Lowlands, John Knox's plan for a school in every parish had broadly been accomplished before the Industrial Revolution. Parliament passed Acts to establish schools, in 1696 and 1803 for example, but the cost of building the school and paying the master's salary fell on the local landowners.

In 1872 the Government agreed to pay for a national system of elementary education in Scotland. School boards were elected to build and manage the schools in each parish, and a great many new schools were built at this time. All children from five to 13 had to attend school to learn 'the three Rs' (reading, writing and arithmetic).

Since then the scope of education has widened. Now children attend primary schools from the age of five to 12 years and then pass on to secondary schools.

Carving on the old Dean Village School, Edinburgh

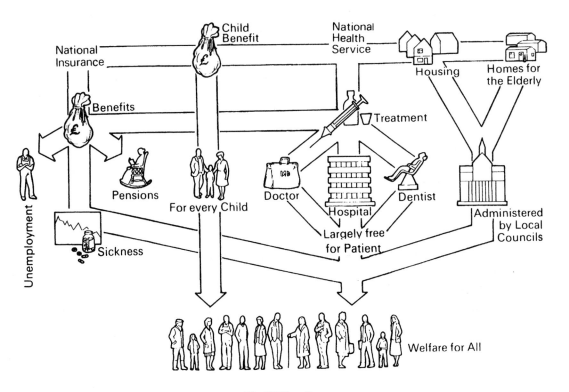

The Welfare State

When they leave school to take a job they usually have further education courses or training at technical colleges. Others go on to universities or colleges. Education is free in nearly all schools and books are provided. Grants have helped pupils to stay at school beyond the legal leaving age of 16 and to become students at universities and colleges. Increasingly, however, students are having to take out loans to pay more of the cost of maintaining themselves while studying and are now faced with fees of up to £1,000 a year for the teaching they receive. This is bound to discourage young people of ability, especially from poorer families, from entering courses at universities.

The Welfare State

Before 1914 the Liberal government, which could count on the votes of most Scottish people, set out to help the old, the sick and the unemployed. In 1908 the first old-age pensions were paid: five shillings (25p) a week for a single person over 70, seven and sixpence ($37^1/_2$p) for a married couple. The amount does not seem much to us now, but wages were much lower then and this was the beginning of a fairer deal for the worker in his old age. Three years later, Lloyd George, a

217

colourful Welsh lawyer who later became Prime Minister, introduced the National Insurance Act to help the worker in times of sickness and unemployment.

In the health scheme each worker paid fourpence a week, his employer threepence, and the State twopence. For his fourpence he was going to get ninepence worth of cover – ten shillings (50p) a week sickness benefit in addition to free medical attention. Some people objected to the scheme because part of the cost had to come out of taxation. To pay for it Lloyd George imposed heavier taxes on the rich. He was behaving like a twentieth-century Robin Hood.

Some workers and the firms they worked for had also to share the cost of a plan to pay them unemployment benefit when there was no work for them. After 1945 the Labour Government, led by Clement Attlee, extended these rights of unemployment benefit, sickness benefit and pensions to everyone in the country. These measures made Britain a 'Welfare State'.

Since then the benefits and services the Welfare State supplies have been improved and extended. The worker and his employer both help to pay for his national insurance, but most of the cost is met from taxes such as income tax. In the case of the Health Service in Scotland, for example, something like 85 per cent of the cost comes from national taxation and in 1995–96 its total cost in Scotland was over £4.3 billion. The Health Service is also one of the biggest employers in Scotland with a workforce of 120,000, more than half of whom are nurses. This means that one worker out of every 19 in Scotland is now involved in some way in the Health Service – a very different situation from earlier centuries when doctors were few and most people were too poor to afford medical care.

In addition, social services for children and the elderly, pensions, and benefits for the sick and the unemployed, give people far more security than they could possibly provide for themselves. Older people in Scotland whose only income is their retirement pension, however, like those people out of work, find life hard.

According to figures published in November 1997, the number of people who are unemployed and claiming benefit in Britain fell to its lowest level for 17 years. The official figure for Scotland – 146,700 unemployed and claiming benefit – does not give a true picture of the men and women who do not have a job, however, since many of them are not counted because they do not qualify for benefit.

42

Government and the People

1997 marked the forty-fifth year of the reign of Queen Elizabeth II and I of Scotland. The Queen reigns but does not rule in the way that earlier kings and queens did. Real power is exercised in her name by 'Her Majesty's Government'.

The government has many tasks. It is responsible for relations with other countries and keeps armed forces for defence. It has to maintain law and order at home by means of the police and the law courts. It has tried to do more for people's welfare, either by giving money to people who are unemployed or sick, and pensions to the elderly, or through the National Health Service. The government also meets most of the expense of education. All these services cost a great deal of money. They are paid for out of the taxes people pay or else by government borrowing.

If the government were above the people and could not be thrown out by them, the system of government would be called 'tyranny', even if the laws it passed were for the benefit of the people. In Britain today the government has to have the support of the majority (more than half) of the members of the House of Commons, who have been elected by the people. If it loses their support, it loses the right to govern. The party which defeats it may take over and govern or else there will be a general election. This system of government is called 'democracy'.

Electing a Member of Parliament

Parliament makes laws and agrees to taxes. There are two Houses of Parliament, the House of Commons and the House of Lords. The House of Commons is the more important House and its members are elected every five years. The country is divided into 635 areas called 'constituencies', which each elect one member to represent it in the House of Commons.

Every man and women over the age of 18 has the right to cast one vote. Many people in Britain belong to political parties such as the Conservatives, Labour, Liberal Democrats and the Greens, and in Scotland the Scottish Nationalist Party as well. Each party has its own ideas about what is best for the country. In a constituency each party may put up a candidate or a person may stand as an Independent. Let us imagine that these four people are candidates in a constituency in a general election:

James Black	W Party
Margaret Brown	X Party
Anne Gray	Y Party
William White	Z Party

On election day the voters go and cast their votes in secret. When the votes have been counted the result is announced:

James Black	6,002 votes
Margaret Brown	14,924 votes
Anne Gray	257 votes
William White	18,561 votes

Having won more votes than any of the other candidates, William White becomes MP for the constituency, even though the votes for the other three candidates combined are greater than his own. Such is the present 'first past the post' system.

Prime Minister and Cabinet

William White's victory is also a victory for his party. If the Z party wins 318 or more of the seats in the House of Commons, it will have more than all the other parties put together and its leader will become head of the government as Prime Minister. He, or she, chooses the team of ministers called the Cabinet from MPs of the same party. Each minister takes charge of one branch of the government, such as finance or foreign affairs.

With the majority in the House of Commons, the Prime Minister and the Cabinet become the government for the next five years. Everything they do, however, can be criticised the next day by MPs and the newspapers. Every law they propose, every change in taxation or spending has to be defended in the House and can take effect only after the majority of MPs have voted in favour of them. The government has also to bear in mind that everything it does will be judged by the voters at the next general election. Even so, once a government has gained power in recent times, it has proved extremely difficult to remove.

Scotland's Special Place in Britain

One of the members of the Cabinet is the Secretary of State for Scotland. Being responsible for Scottish development, education, health, housing, social work, roads, agriculture and fisheries, he is practically 'Prime Minister for Scottish matters'. In the Cabinet he is also expected to press Scotland's case for more money or better roads.

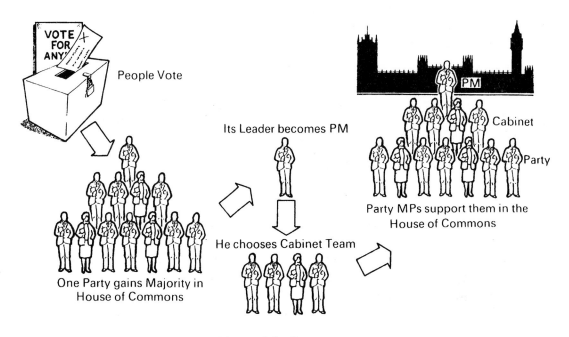

Voters and the Government

Even in the 1950s when Scottish voters divided their support almost equally between the two main British political parties, Conservatives and Labour, many people felt that their MPs had too few opportunities to question the Secretary of State for Scotland on his wide range of responsibilities. This was because the British Parliament in which they sit in London would not give more time to matters which are of interest to Scottish people only.

With shipyards and coalmines closing and much of its traditional heavy industry in decline, Scottish voters won Scotland for Labour in 1964 taking 44 Labour seats to the Conservatives' 24. These Labour victories in Scotland gave the Labour party under Harold Wilson power in Britain, even although its majority in the whole of Britain was only three. This was the beginning of a trend of Scotland consistently returning a large majority of Labour MPs at every election.

The reward the Labour government gave Scotland in the 1960s was a national plan, to modernise the country and attract new industries by spending 20 per cent more per head in Scotland than the British average. The Conservatives, on the other hand, began to consider 'devolution', that is that an elected assembly in Edinburgh take some part in making laws for Scotland; a mild measure not likely to silence the discontent in Scotland. The Scottish National Party, whose ultimate aim is independence, claimed that Scotland could soon be a rich and independent country if the oil being brought ashore from the North Sea could be reserved for Scotland's special benefit. 'It's Scotland's Oil' was the cry in 1972; the SNP won seven seats in the election in February 1974 and won 11 seats and 30 per cent of all the votes cast – more than the Conservatives – in October the same year.

In 1978 the Labour government passed the Scotland Act to set up a Scottish Assembly (or parliament) to meet in Edinburgh. This Act would give the Assembly the power to make laws and decisions on most of the Scottish affairs for which the Secretary of State for Scotland was formerly responsible. These powers would be 'devolved', that is, handed down from the United Kingdom Parliament in London to the Scottish Assembly in Edinburgh. At the same time, Scottish voters would continue to elect other MPs for the United Kingdom Parliament, to deal with matters of common interest such as defence. This Act offered them more self-government without breaking the Treaty of Union of 1707.

In a special public vote, or referendum, on 1 March 1979, too few voted in favour and the General Election which followed resulted in a change of Government and Margaret Thatcher, leader of the Conservative party, became Britain's first woman Prime Minister.

On the strength of their majority in Britain and in spite of the small number of Scotland's MPs who belong to their party (only 10 out of 72 in 1996), the Conservatives carried on governing Scotland. They insisted that they stood for the United Kingdom and that the Union brought Scotland great benefits. The Scottish Nationalists, gaining support especially from young people, reject this and are striving towards making Scotland an independent nation, running its own affairs.

Between these two extremes *A Claim of Right for Scotland* was drawn up in 1988, stating the constitutional rights Scotland expected within the United Kingdom. It had a broad appeal and led to Labour and Liberal Democrat MPs and others working together to hammer out proposals (published as *Scotland's Parliament, Scotland's Right* on St Andrew's Day 1995) for a Scottish Parliament. This body would deal with Scottish affairs in Scotland, inside the framework of the United Kingdom. To the surprise of many, however, the Conservatives held on to power in the 1992 General Election but their proposals for increasing the Secretary of State's powers without creating a Scottish Assembly did not satisfy many Scottish people. In the General Election of 1997 they were defeated in every constituency in Scotland. Labour, back in power in Britain for the first time in 18 years, immediately introduced a Bill to set up a Scottish Parliament. Asked for their opinion in a referendum on 11 September 1997, Scots voted overwhelmingly in favour of a Scottish Parliament with the right to raise or lower taxes. This was a great day for Scotland, bringing control of Scottish affairs closer to the people.

Local Government

The great reform in local government in 1975 abolished all the town councils and county councils in Scotland and created bigger, but fewer, councils. Most power in local affairs was handed over to the nine regional councils to provide all the main services – planning, education, social work, police and roads for all the people in the region. For more local needs each region was divided into districts, each with a district council, providing housing and cleansing, libraries and parks. Only the islanders in the west and north received all their services from their single island council.

Most of the money to pay for local services comes from grants from the government out of general taxation. The contribution people make locally used to be based on the value of the house a family lived in. The attempt in 1988, a year earlier than the rest of the UK, to make every adult in Scotland pay an equal share of community charge instead, called the 'poll tax' by its enemies, proved so unpopular that it had to be abandoned. The council tax, which replaced it, was again based on the value of a family's house, with a discount for householders living alone.

Some of the regions were big and powerful. Strathclyde, the biggest, governed 45 per cent of the people of Scotland. Lothian controlled another 15 per cent and both had Labour majorities. The government, Conservative with not a lot of support in Scotland, proposed a further reform of local government in 1993 – to abolish all 62 regional and district councils and to set up 28 all-purpose authorities, where a single council would provide all the services in its area, as the island councils had done. The first elections for the new councils in April 1995 proved a disaster for the Conservatives who failed to gain control of even one council in Scotland.

The old Royal High School, Edinburgh, converted and now called New Parliament House,
the focus of people's hopes for a Scottish Parliament since 1979

43

Famous Scots at Home and Abroad

Nations, small nations especially, are proud when their sons and daughters achieve great things, and the Scots are certainly no exception.

Science and Medicine

In science James Hutton studied rocks in the eighteenth century and laid the foundations of the study of geology, while Hugh Miller (1802–56), a stonemason from Cromarty, aroused popular interest in geology through his books *The Old Red Sandstone* and *The Testimony of the Rocks*. By experimenting, James Young succeeded in producing paraffin from the shale deposits in West Lothian and started a new industry, until a million gallons of paraffin for heating and lighting were being produced every year.

Discovering chloroform in 1847, by using it on himself, James Young Simpson was able not only to free patients from pain but to give surgeons much more time to perform operations. Surgery was a man's world, however, and hospitals were very slow to admit women as doctors. In 1901 Doctor Elsie Inglis started a maternity hospital in Edinburgh where all of the staff were women; the memorial hospital named after her (closed in 1988) is held in deep affection by former patients.

In 1928 a Scottish medical researcher, Alexander Fleming, discovered a mould, which he called penicillin. Once others had discovered how to produce it, penicillin became something of a wonder drug in the treatment of infectious diseases after the Second World War. John Boyd Orr, on the other hand, believed that the greatest problem facing the world was how to grow enough food to feed its ever-increasing population. Author of *Food and the People* in 1944, he was a good choice to tackle it when he was appointed the first Director of the United Nations Food and Agriculture Organisation in 1945.

In the nineteenth century Lord Kelvin, who was born in Ireland but spent nearly all of his long life in Glasgow, made many advances: improving the compasses on ships, supervising the laying of the first cable under the Atlantic, and pioneering electric light in Glasgow. It was Alexander Graham Bell, a Scotsman in the United States, who first sent a message over a distance by telephone and set up his own company, the Bell Telephone Company.

Politics

In British politics during the last hundred years several Scots have been prime minister, but for fairly short periods only: Lord Rosebery (1894–95) and Henry Campbell-Bannerman (1905–8) for the Liberals; A.J. Balfour (1902–6), Andrew Bonar Law (1922–23) and Sir Alec Douglas Home (1963–64) for the Conservatives; and Ramsay MacDonald (1924 and 1929–31) for Labour and then from 1931 to 1935 as head of a National Government, which was almost entirely Conservative. Since the War, Jo Grimond and David Steel have both been leaders of the Liberal party, while John Smith, a Labour minister in the 1970s who became leader of the party in Britain in 1992, looked likely to become the next Prime Minister of Great Britain until his untimely death in 1994.

Art and Architecture

Allan Ramsay (1713–84), famous for the delicate portrait of his wife, Margaret Lindsay, and Henry Raeburn (1756–1823) were great Scottish portrait painters. Thanks to them we know what many well known Scots of their day looked like: David Hume, painted by Ramsay, for example, and Sir Walter Scott by Raeburn.

Hill House, Helensburgh, by Charles Rennie Mackintosh

The famous portrait of Robert Burns, on the other hand, is by Alexander Nasmyth. A little later David Wilkie became noted for his scenes of Scottish life: from *Pitlessie Fair*, painted when he was only 19, to *Reading the Will* and *The Letter of Introduction*, when he was in his prime. In 1890 William McTaggart painted *The Storm*, probably the finest among his many seascapes. Of the many twentieth century painters, the work of two women, Anne Redpath and Joan Eardley, has become highly regarded in recent years; Redpath for interiors in the richest of colours and Eardley, though born in England, for her studies of Glasgow children and, like McTaggart, her efforts to capture on canvas the power of the raging sea.

The greatest Scottish name among architects is undoubtedly Robert Adam (1728–92) whose neo-classical style, the result of his studies of Roman ruins in Italy, can be seen at its best in country houses like Mellerstain in Berwickshire, the University of Edinburgh (now called Old College) on South Bridge, and the Register House at the east end of Princes Street in Edinburgh. In his plans for a house, Adam believed in designing everything, including the furniture and the door handles. So did Charles Rennie Mackintosh (1868–1928) whose houses on the outside show the influence of traditional Scottish buildings on him, whereas in their decoration, fabrics and furniture for the inside, he and his wife Margaret pioneered a new style called Art Nouveau which proved very popular in Europe.

Writers

Robert Burns, Scotland's national poet, (*see* page 173) and Sir Walter Scott are the two Scottish writers who are best known overseas – Burns for his poems such as 'Tam o' Shanter' and songs like 'Ae fond kiss', and Scott for his *Waverley Novels*, which have given so many readers their ideas about Scotland and its history. In the 1880s Robert Louis Stevenson also won fame for his novels, notably *Treasure Island* and *Kidnapped*, and 50 years later Lewis Grassic Gibbon wrote *Sunset Song*, a classic tale of country life in the north-east of Scotland.

Among poets this century Hugh MacDiarmid led the way towards the use of Scottish words and phrases as the language of his poetry while Sorley MacLean became widely recognised as the greatest poet in his native Gaelic.

Sport

From St Andrews, 'home of golf', came Tom Morris, 'Old Tom', who won the British championship four times between 1861 and 1866 and his son 'Young Tom' who won it three years in succession. Scotland produces many good golfers still, including Sandy Lyle who won the British Open Championship in 1985 and more recently Colin Montgomerie.

In football Scotland also finds its heroes and they are usually goal-scorers – Denis Law, Kenny Dalglish and in the 1980s and '90s, Ally McCoist. Dalglish went on to become a successful manager in England, like other Scots: Matt Busby with Manchester United and Bill Shankly with Liverpool. Inside Scotland, Jock Stein was the greatest Scottish football manager, his club Celtic winning the Scottish championship time and again, and the European Cup in 1967. Thanks to his footballing brain and extreme fitness, Gordon Strachan has been an inspiring general on the field, first of all for Aberdeen and often for Scotland.

In rugby Andy Irvine, fullback for Heriots and for Scotland, was probably the most exciting player in the last 50 years. Border half-backs John Rutherford and Roy Laidlaw played together 35 times for the Scotland XV which won the Grand Slam in 1984, while Gavin Hastings, another fullback, has been an inspiring captain of Scotland, and of the British Lions in New Zealand in 1993.

In athletics Allan Wells won the gold medal in the 100m sprint in the Olympic Games in Moscow in 1980 and was second in the 200m, while Tom McKean has won the European Cup in the 800m no less than four times. Scottish women have been more successful over longer distances, Yvonne Murray winning the European Championship in 1990 over 3,000 metres and the Commonwealth Championship in 1994 in the 10,000 metres; while Liz McColgan won the Commonwealth gold medal in 1986 and 1990, the World Championship in 1991 over 10,000 metres, and broke the world record in 1993.

The first World Sevens Cup tournament, held at Murrayfield, 1993

Abroad

'Go into whatever country you will', wrote Edward Topham, an English visitor to Edinburgh in 1775, 'you will always find Scotchmen . . . They penetrate into every climate: you meet them in all the various departments of travellers, soldiers, merchants, adventurers, domestics . . . If any new countries [have been] visited and improved, a Scotchman has borne some share in the performance'.

Explorers

If this was true in Topham's time, how much truer it has become over the 200 years since then. Scots have played a part adding to our geographical knowledge of different parts of the world, for example. In the north of Canada, Alexander Mackenzie from Stornoway, discovered the Mackenzie River in 1789 and followed it north-west to the Arctic Ocean. In Australia Allan Cunningham, who came from Renfrewshire, discovered the Darling Downs, excellent grazing for sheep; and in 1838 Thomas Mitchell, a soldier from Stirlingshire, published his surveys of the vast, attractive area watered by the Murray and the Darling Rivers, which led to many Scots going out to settle there. Very different was the expedition of John McDouall Stuart in 1861 from Adelaide in South Australia, who just survived the intense heat and the drought in the centre to reach the sea at last in the north.

Others looked for the sources of great rivers in Africa. Mungo Park, trying to find the source of the Niger, was drowned when attacked by natives in 1806 but 20 years later it was discovered by Alexander G. Laing, another Scotsman. Earlier in 1770 James Bruce reached the source of the Blue Nile. James A. Grant was on J.H. Speke's expedition in 1864, exploring the sources of the Nile and wrote an account of his travels which he called *A Walk Across Africa*. Farther south David Livingstone, from Blantyre in Lanarkshire, became a missionary and explorer. 'I am willing to go anywhere', he once said, 'provided it be forward'. He explored the Zambezi and discovered the Victoria Falls and went on to explore the great lakes Nyasa and Tanganyika.

Missionaries

Inspired by Livingstone, Mary Slessor (1848–1915), a mill-girl from Dundee, risked death from malaria, which killed so many, to work as a missionary among the forest tribes near Calabar in West Africa, which she did for nearly 40 years.

Eric Liddell (1902–45), who may be better known as the runner who gave up the chance of winning an Olympic gold medal in the 100 metres because he would have had to run on a Sunday, was a missionary in China for 20 years and died in a Japanese prison camp. His story as a runner lives on in the outstanding film *Chariots of Fire*.

Politics

Lachlan Macquarie was an outstanding Governor of New South Wales (1810–21) who turned its convict settlement into a forward-looking civil state by building roads, schools and churches and by giving freed prisoners the chance to make a new life for themselves, even in the government service. He has been called 'The Father of Australia'. Nearly a century later a former Ayrshire miner, Andrew Fisher, became the leader of the Australian Labour Party and was Prime Minister of Australia three times between 1908 and 1915. Robert Stout from Shetland helped to make trade unions legal in New Zealand and was Prime Minister from 1884–87. In Canada, John A. MacDonald was the first Prime Minister when the states in Canada joined together in the Dominion of Canada in 1867.

Two Scots in the United States

Andrew Carnegie (1835–1918), a poor weaver's son from Dunfermline, rose to dominate the steel industry in America. He made his fortune, but he believed that 'to die rich was to die disgraced' and gave away millions to provide public libraries in towns all over Britain and the US, as well as donating hundreds of organs to churches in many countries, and gifts to Scottish universities and his home town, Dunfermline. John Muir (1838–1914) from Dunbar was overwhelmed by the

Muir Woods in California, named in 1908 to honour John Muir's conservation work in the US

beauty he saw in the untouched wilderness in California – the mountains, the animals, the plants, the trees. He made it his life's work to protect them and he succeeded: the National Parks in the US have had the duty since 1890 to protect them for all time. So far Scotland has no National Parks but people here, touched by John Muir's message, are also beginning to care.

Visits

The Scottish National Portrait Gallery in Queen Street, Edinburgh, is the best place to start, because of its large collection of pictures of famous Scots. Around the entrance hall you'll also see the panorama by William Hole of well-known figures from every age, as if walking through Scottish history.

Again in Edinburgh, visit the National Gallery on the Mound, close to Princes Street, to view Scottish paintings. To learn about Scottish writers – Burns, Scott and Stevenson – visit the Writers Museum at the top of the Mound. Burns' Cottage at Alloway in Ayrshire, of course, is a place of pilgrimage, and his house and the Robert Burns Centre in Dumfries are both interesting, while Sir Walter Scott's house at Abbotsford, near Galashiels, is full of historical treasures he collected.

For James Watt and Lord Kelvin, visit the Hunterian Museum, Gilmorehill, University of Glasgow; while the Art Gallery opposite is a good introduction to Charles Rennie Mackintosh, whose Hill House at Helensburgh, which can be accessed by rail from Queen Street Station, is a wonderful example of his style.

For Mary Slessor visit Dundee City Museum, McManus Gallery, Nethergate; and for David Livingstone the centre named after him at Blantyre, near Hamilton in Lanarkshire.

Plaque outside Andrew Carnegie's birthplace, Dunfermline

44

In Modern Scotland

We have seen how people's lives in Scotland have changed through the ages. We have come a long way from Stone Age people, who had to supply all their needs by their own efforts. In early times life changed very, very slowly. Since the beginning of the Industrial Revolution the pace has quickened. The development of heavy industries – coal mining, iron and steel, engineering, ship-building, locomotive-building – stimulated the growth of towns in central Scotland until four out of five Scots were living in towns. Since their dramatic decline in the last 20 years, the work they provided has gone yet most of the people remain.

Two other factors are worth remembering when considering Scotland today: the number of casualties suffered in the First World War (1914–18) and the extent of emigration from Scotland in the nineteenth and twentieth centuries. It has been estimated that over 100,000 Scots, the flower of their generation, were killed in that war, a figure much higher than the average for Britain as a whole. The tragedy of this can be appreciated by visiting the National War Memorial in Edinburgh Castle or looking at the long lists of names on war memorials in country places where few people live now. The island of Raasay, for example, has a population of only 150 today and out of 36 of the men who went off to war, 22 were killed, two of them at the age of only 17.

Secondly, emigration in great numbers began amidst the distress caused by the potato famine in 1846, when people left the Western Isles and West Highlands for Canada, the United States and, to a lesser extent, Australia, and it continued due to later famines. Probably about 60,000 went away between 1846 and 1861, and in many cases landlords paid their passages, being relieved to see them go. In the next 60 years from 1860 to 1919, nearly another 60,000 were attracted to emigrate to Australia through special assistance schemes,

The call to arms in 1914, in Princes Street Gardens, Edinburgh

but most of these emigrants were from the south and east of Scotland. Soon chains of migration were established and younger relatives were encouraged to follow their example and try their luck in a growing young country. The habit continues. While the total population of Scotland remains stubbornly steady at a little above five million, it has been calculated that over two million Scots left Scotland during the twentieth century alone.

Workers and Work

The kinds of jobs people do to earn a living have changed a great deal. By 1995 the number of workers that farmers employed on their farms was down to 25,500 compared with almost 120,000 in 1921. Today there are far more teachers than there are farm workers. Engineering is the main industry employing about 125,000 workers, a fall of a third in 12 years. Generally, improvements in machinery have reduced the number of workers needed to grow food on farms or to make goods in factories, while more people work in transporting goods or selling them. Nearly a quarter of a million other workers are employed by local government; for example, typists, social workers, teachers, firemen and refuse collectors. They all provide a service which helps people in some way. Another important change has been the large increase in the number of women employed, but four out of every ten women workers work part-time.

People in work enjoy a higher standard of living than ever before, and are

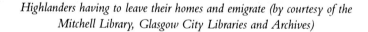

Highlanders having to leave their homes and emigrate (by courtesy of the Mitchell Library, Glasgow City Libraries and Archives)

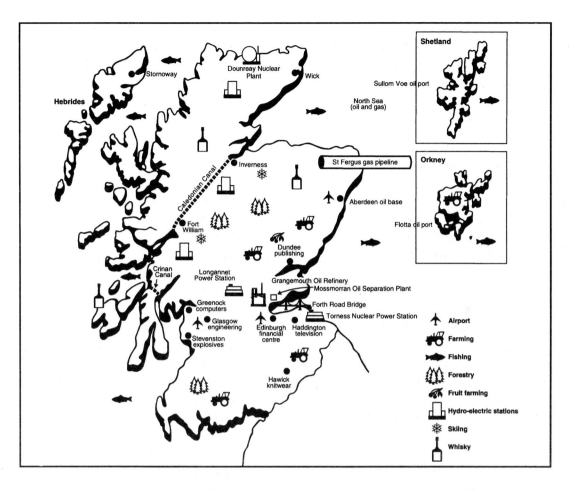

Industrial Scotland

protected against unemployment and ill-health. They work at a greater pace than their grandparents did but heavy labour has been eased by the use of machinery and hours of work are much shorter. They also have more leisure time.

While the number of people in work has been rising steadily, in October 1997 over 146,000 men and women did not share in this general improvement because they could not find paid employment, and for young people leaving school rewarding jobs are scarce.

Planning and New Industries

In the early years of the Industrial Revolution no one controlled how industries grew up or how big they became. For far too long, too many Scottish workers were employed in the older, heavy industries – coal, steel, shipbuilding – and

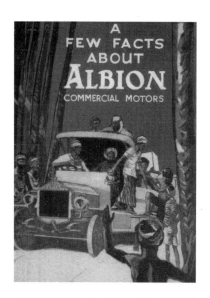

Albion Motors, who claimed in 1921 to be 'the largest manufacturers of motor vans in the British Empire' (courtesy of Albion Archive, Biggar Museum Trust)

when these could not produce as cheaply as their competitors in the 1970s and 1980s, Scotland had more workers out of work than other parts of Britain.

Many new jobs were created in new industries, however, by making detailed plans and spending large sums of money. The whole of Scotland, except for an area round Aberdeen, was made a Development Area for a time, and firms setting up factories qualified for grants from the government to help them to pay for new buildings and new machinery. It is estimated that this kind of help created ten thousand new jobs every year in the 1960s. In five New Towns in particular – East Kilbride, Glenrothes, Cumbernauld, Irvine and Livingston – everything was planned: where the factories were to be, compared with the houses; how many houses to build each year; what kind of factories and workshops to provide; what were the other services that people needed, things like schools and churches, shops and community centres. With the exception of Aberdeen, the oil capital of Britain, the new towns have attracted many of the high-technology industries which have turned Central Scotland into 'Silicon Glen'. Of the personal computers now sold in Europe, 40 per cent are manufactured in Scotland.

Since then when large industries have collapsed, like the Singer Sewing Machine Company in Clydebank in 1980, for example, with the loss of 3,000 jobs, policy changed under the Conservatives and the Clydebank area became an Enterprise Zone. Factories and workshops were built and firms were attracted to set up businesses inside the zone, knowing that they would be free of the commercial rates their rivals had to pay outside. Other areas also became Enterprise Zones: Invergordon where the aluminium smelter closed in 1981, Tayside centred on Dundee, and Inverclyde centred on Greenock.

In the early days of motoring, several cars – the Albion, the Argyll and the Arrol-Johnston – were built in Scotland but none of them in great numbers. Scotland did not have a share of the modern motor industry until the 1960s when the assembly of tractors and trucks began at Bathgate and of cars at Linwood near Paisley. But these were always 'branch factories', branches of big firms whose centres were elsewhere, and when hard times came, it was the branches which closed. Early in 1993 when Leyland Daf, the truck maker in England collapsed, Albion Motors, its supplier and one of the last remnants of the motor industry in Scotland, was left fighting to survive.

Planning to bring new industries to the Highlands began as early as the Second

World War when Thomas Johnston, the Labour MP for West Stirling, accepted Winston Churchill's invitation to become Secretary of State for Scotland. Johnston strengthened his independence from the government in London by refusing to draw any salary as Scottish Secretary and by gathering former Secretaries of State into a Council of Ministers to work with him. With their backing he took the first steps towards Highland water power producing electricity for homes and factories, more employment opportunities in forestry and fishing, and the creation of the Scottish Tourist Board.

In 1965 the Highlands and Islands Development Board was set up to build on Johnston's foundations to help to provide work to keep Highland people in the Highlands. Larger enterprises, such as the aluminium smelter at Invergordon, have not always proved long-lasting but with the Board's help many smaller businesses have been established in factories, craft workshops, and fish farms, besides all the facilities catering for visitors. The extensive network of tourist information centres in the Highlands became a boon for travellers, giving assistance on where to stay and what to see and do. The Board was replaced in 1990 by Highlands and Islands Enterprise, and smaller areas also have their own Enterprise Companies. A measure of the Board's success is that population in the Highlands rose by one-eighth in the 1970s, and by one per cent between 1981 and 1988 whereas the population in Scotland as a whole showed a small decline in the same period. Highland population continues to increase but only very slowly.

Energy

Homes and factories use much less coal directly than they did in the past and the output of coal in 1990 fell to 7 million tonnes, with Longannet in West Fife the only coalmine left supplying coal to produce electricity today. In the Highlands, water power creates electricity and there are nuclear power stations at Hunterston and Torness.

Natural gas from the North Sea is another source of energy. In 1978 gas from the Frigg field began to flow to the terminal at St Fergus, on the coast north of Aberdeen, and south to its customers through a pipeline nearly 1,300 kilometres long. Further supplies of gas have been found in association with oil and piped ashore.

The most exciting result of exploring the North Sea has been the discovery of oil in large quantities. Oil companies moved quickly to install production platforms and lay pipelines. Aberdeen became the oil capital and boom town of Britain as workers flocked in to jobs connected with oil and by 1989 60,000 workers in Scotland were employed in the oil industry. The first oil was brought ashore from the little Argyll field in 1975 and production built up so quickly that in 1988 114 million tonnes of oil were brought ashore from 43 oil fields. The result of this has been that not only Scotland but the whole of the United Kingdom became self-sufficient in oil as early as 1980. Production reached a peak of 2.7 million barrels a day in 1985 and has been running at nearly 2 million barrels a day for many years. In October 1995 oil and gas output was at a new peak and a year later they were together worth £54 million every day. Even in 1994, oil exports were worth over £4 billion. This made the UK (in fact, Scotland) the second biggest offshore oil producer in the world, after Saudi Arabia, and new discoveries in the Atlantic at a deeper level west of Shetland suggest reserves of 3.5 billion barrels.

But the oil will not last for ever. As a resource it is beyond price and it ought to be drawn on at a controlled rate which takes heed of the interests of people in the future as much as the present. The sudden riches oil brought gave Britain the opportunity to use this wealth to invest in new industries and re-equip older ones to provide satisfying jobs for more people – but it has not been taken.

The construction stage of building huge production platforms has passed, making many workers unemployed. The nature of the materials – oil and gas; the place – out in the North Sea; and the uncertainty of the weather combine to make the extraction of oil a dangerous occupation. The tragic fire on the Piper Alpha platform proved this in 1988 when 170 workers lost their lives. The other danger is pollution of the coast and the sea, which happened in January 1993, when the *Braer*, carrying 85,000 tonnes of light crude oil from Norway, broke up on the rocks of south Shetland. Heavy seas dispersed the oil quickly but the long-term effects are still unknown.

Sullom Voe oil port in Shetland

45

Conclusion: A Time of Hope

Two events in 1997 – the Labour Party's overwhelming victory in the General Election on 1 May and Scotland's decisive 'Yes, Yes' vote for devolution on 11 September, herald a new era in the government of Scotland.

First, the Labour government is the first British government for eighteen years to have the support of the majority of Scottish people. The new Secretary of State for Scotland, Donald Dewar, is effectively responsible for running the country, and for the first time in eighteen years he is able to carry out his role with the majority of Scottish MPs supporting him – like him, most are members of the Labour Party.

Secondly, in the campaign for a Scottish Parliament with tax-varying powers within the framework of the United Kingdom, Labour had the support of the Liberal Democrats and the Scottish Nationalists. In an historic moment, the Scottish people came together and showed that they believed in themselves.

For the first time since the Act of Union of 1707, Scotland will have (from the year 2000) its own Parliament with time to discuss its own affairs. It will have power to make laws and decide how best to spend money on a wide range of services – health; schools and higher education; law, the courts and the police; local government, social work and housing; industry, trade and transport; agriculture, the environment and fisheries; as well as sport and the arts – all matters close to the needs of the people.

Scotland will continue to have MPs in the British Parliament, which will deal with finance, economic policy and taxation; foreign policy and defence; and employment and social security for the whole of the United Kingdom, including Scotland.

Scottish ministers and officials can expect to play an increasing role along with their UK colleagues in relations with the European Union. Scotland will be able to deal directly with its institutions and already has eight members in the European Parliament. Its historic links with Europe, which began even before the Auld Alliance of 1295 and developed until the Union of 1707 when Scotland ceased to be an independent nation, seem primed for future renewal.

Meanwhile, inside Scotland interest in all things Scottish has been increasing. There are signs of a growing national consciousness which is coinciding with the prospect of a Scottish Parliament being able to create a fairer and a better Scotland. This is an exciting time, a time of hope.

Index

(Italics signify names of battles)